TEACHER'S PET PUBLICATIONS

LITPLAN TEACHER PACK
for
The Secret Life of Bees

based on the novel by
Sue Monk Kidd

Written by
Catherine Caldwell & Mary B. Collins

TABLE OF CONTENTS
The Secret Life Of Bees

Introduction	6
Unit Objectives	8
Reading Assignment Sheet	9
Unit Outline	10
Study Questions (Short Answer)	13
Quiz/Study Questions (Multiple Choice)	27
Pre-reading Vocabulary Worksheets	55
Lesson One (Introductory Lesson)	81
Oral Reading Evaluation Form	88
Writing Assignment 1	113
Writing Evaluation Form	114
Nonfiction Assignment Sheet	83
Writing Assignment 2	118
Writing Assignment 3	122
Extra Writing Assignments/Discussion ?s	153
Vocabulary Review Activities	156
Unit Review Activities	157
Unit Tests	163
Unit Resource Materials	225
Vocabulary Resource Materials	249

ABOUT THE AUTHOR

Sue Monk Kidd

Sue Monk Kidd was born on August 12, 1948 in Sylvester, Georgia. In 1970 she graduated from Texas Christian University with a B. S. in nursing.

In the mid-to-late 1970's she enrolled in writing classes and started getting published as a freelance writer, writing mostly personal experience articles. She became contributing editor of *Guideposts Magazine*.

Sue's first books were spiritual memoirs published by Harper SanFrancisco: *God's Joyful Surprise* (1988), *When the Heart Waits* (1990), and *The Dance of the Dissident Daughter* (1996).

In 1997 she began her first work of fiction, *The Secret Life of Bees*, which was published by Viking in 2002. Her second novel, *The Mermaid Chair*, was published in 2005.

Sue Monk Kidd lives by a salt marsh near Charleston, South Carolina with her husband Sandy and a black lab named Lily.

Awards

2006 Distinguished Alumna of the Year, presented by Texas Christian University

2006 South Carolina "The Order of the Palmetto" Award - The state's highest civilian honor, bestowed by the Governor

2005 Winner of the Quill Award in General Fiction - *The Mermaid Chair*

2005 Southeastern Library Association Fiction Award winner - *The Secret Life of Bees*

2004 Book Sense Book of the Year in paperback - *The Secret Life of Bees*

Recipient of the inaugural Literature To Life award presented by The American Place Theatre, New York, NY- 2004

Nominated for the 2004 International IMPAC Dublin Literary Award (Dublin, Ireland) for *The Secret Life of Bees*

Winner of the 2003 SEBA Book of the Year for *The Secret Life of Bees*

Finalist for the 2003 Book Sense Book of the Year Award for fiction - *The Secret Life of Bees*

Finalist for the 2003 Boeke Prize in South Africa for *The Secret Life of Bees*

Nominated for the 2002 Orange Prize in England for *The Secret Life of Bees*

Winner of the 1996 Poets & Writers Exchange Program in Fiction for South Carolina

1993-1994 South Carolina Fellowship in Literature (Fiction) by the South Carolina Arts Commission

Citation in "100 Distinguished Stories" by Best American Short Stories 1994 for *The*

Secret Life of Bees

Citation in "100 Distinguished Stories" by Best American Short Stories 1996 for *In the Graveyard of Afterbirth*

1993 Katherine Anne Porter Second Prize in Fiction by the Nimrod/Hardman Awards

1994 and 1996 South Carolina Academy of Authors Fellowships in Fiction by the S.C. Academy of Authors

1993, 1995 and 1997 South Carolina Fiction Project Winner by the South Carolina Arts Commission/ Charleston Post and Courier

1995 Bread Loaf Scholar in fiction, Bread Loaf Writers Conference, Middlebury, VT

Named to the 1994, 1995, and 1996 South Carolina Readers Circuit

1994 Isak Dineson Creative Non-Fiction Award

1999 Literal Latte Creative Non-Fiction third prize

INTRODUCTION *The Secret Life of Bees*

This LitPlan has been designed to develop students' reading, writing, thinking, and language skills through exercises and activities related to *The Secret Life of Bees.* It includes twenty-two lessons, supported by extra resource materials.

In the **introductory lesson** students search for information about topics alluded to in the text, and they are given the materials they will be using during the unit.

The **reading assignments** are approximately thirty pages each; some are a little shorter while others are a little longer. Students have approximately 15 minutes of pre-reading work to do prior to each reading assignment. This pre-reading work involves reviewing the study questions for the assignment and doing some vocabulary work for selected vocabulary words they will encounter in their reading.

The **study guide questions** are fact-based questions; students can find the answers to these questions right in the text. These questions come in two formats: short answer or multiple choice. The best use of these materials is probably to use the short answer version of the questions as study guides for students (since answers will be more complete), and to use the multiple choice version for occasional quizzes.

The **vocabulary work** is intended to enrich students' vocabularies as well as to aid in the students' understanding of the book. Prior to each reading assignment, students will complete a two-part worksheet for selected vocabulary words in the upcoming reading assignment. Part I focuses on students' use of general knowledge and contextual clues by giving the sentence in which the word appears in the text. Students are then to write down what they think the words mean based on the words' usage. Part II nails down the definitions of the words by giving students dictionary definitions of the words and having students match the words to the correct definitions based on the words' contextual usage. Students should then have an understanding of the words when they meet them in the text.

After each reading assignment, students will go back and formulate answers for the study guide questions. Discussion of these questions serves as a **review** of the most important events and ideas presented in the reading assignments.

There is a **vocabulary review** lesson which pulls together all of the fragmented vocabulary lists for the reading assignments and gives students a review of all of the words they have studied.

A lesson is devoted to the **extra discussion questions/writing assignments**. These questions focus on interpretation, critical analysis, and personal response, employing a variety of thinking skills and adding to the students' understanding of the novel.

There is a **group theme project** in this unit. This project requires students to study the text for references to the group's assigned theme, discuss the theme among themselves using a discussion guide, and present information about the theme to the class.

There are three **writing assignments** in this unit, each with the purpose of informing, persuading, or expressing personal opinions. In the first writing assignment students write a short work of historical fiction using a newspaper or magazine article as a basis for their stories. In the second writing assignment students write a letter to send back in time to Lily telling her in detail about an event or topic that was alluded to in the novel. In the third writing assignment students rewrite the scene when T. Ray comes to get Lily from the calendar sisters, from his point of view and persuading Lily to return home with him.

There is a non-fiction **reading assignment**. Students must read non-fiction articles, books, etc. to gather information about topics related to *The Secret Life of Bees*.

The **review lesson** pulls together all of the aspects of the unit. The teacher is given four or five choices of activities or games to use which all serve the same basic function of reviewing all of the information presented in the unit.

The **unit test** comes in two formats: multiple choice or short answer. As a convenience, two different tests for each format have been included. There is also an advanced short answer unit test for advanced students.

There are additional **support materials** included with this unit. The **Unit Resource Materials** section includes suggestions for an in-class library, crossword and word search puzzles related to the novel, and extra worksheets. There is a list of **bulletin board ideas** which gives the teacher suggestions for bulletin boards to go along with this unit. In addition, there is a list of **extra class activities** the teacher could choose from to enhance the unit or as a substitution for an exercise the teacher might feel is inappropriate for his/her class. **Answer keys** are located directly after the **reproducible student materials** throughout the unit. The **Vocabulary Resource Materials** section includes similar worksheets and games to reinforce the vocabulary words.

The **level** of this unit can be varied depending upon the criteria on which the individual assignments are graded, the teacher's expectations of his/her students in class discussions, and the formats chosen for the study guides, quizzes and test. If teachers have other ideas/activities they wish to use, they can usually easily be inserted prior to the review lesson.

UNIT OBJECTIVES *The Secret Life of Bees*

1. Through reading Sue Monk Kidd's *The Secret Life of Bees*, students will explore themes of the novel and make connections between themselves and the larger world.
2. Students will gain a better knowledge of historical events presented in the novel.
3. Students will study the effects of the civil rights movement in the early 1960s.
4. Students will study how the characters cope with the situations life throws at them.
5. Students will study the elements of connotation and denotation, figurative language (onomatopoeia, similie, metaphor, personification, imagery), allusions, epigraphs, and point of view as related to *The Secret Life of Bees*.
6. Students will analyze how literary elements are used to develop the theme of a novel.
7. Students will demonstrate their understanding of the text on four levels: factual, interpretive, critical, and personal.
8. Students will answer questions to demonstrate their understanding of the main events, characters, and ideas in the novel.
9. Students will improve their oral reading skills and individual reading comprehension.
10. Students will enrich their vocabularies and improve their understanding of the novel by using the vocabulary lessons prepared for use in conjunction with the novel.
11. Students will read aloud, report, and participate in large and small group discussions to improve their public speaking and personal interaction skills.
12. The writing assignments are geared to several purposes:
    a. To have students demonstrate their abilities to inform, persuade, express their own personal ideas, or be creative
    b. To check students' reading comprehension
    c. To make students think about ideas presented in the novel
    d. To encourage logical thinking
    e. To provide an opportunity for students to practice good grammar and improve their use of standard, written English

READING ASSIGNMENTS *The Secret Life of Bees*

Date Assigned	Assignment	Completion Date
	Assignment 1 Chapter 1	
	Assignment 2 Chapters 2-3	
	Assignment 3 Chapters 4-5	
	Assignment 4 Chapters 6-7	
	Assignment 5 Chapter 8	
	Assignment 6 Chapter 9	
	Assignment 7 Chapter 10	
	Assignment 8 Chapter 11	
	Assignment 9 Chapter 12	
	Assignment 10 Chapter 13	
	Assignment 11 Chapter 14	

UNIT OUTLINE *The Secret Life of Bees*

1	2	3	4	5
Introduction Allusion Bingo	PVR 1 Oral Reading	Study ?s 1 PVR 2-3 Conotation & Denotation	Study ?s 2-3 PVR 4-5 Characterization	Study ?s 4-5 PVR 6-7 Figurative Language
6 Study ?s 6-7 PVR 8 Allusion	**7** Study ?s 8 PVR 9 Epigraphs	**8** Study ?s 9 PVR 10 Historical Context Purpose & Intent	**9** Writing Assignment #1	**10** Study ?s 10 PVR 11
11 Nonfiction PVR 12	**12** Study ?s 11-12 PVR 13 Writing Assignment #2	**13** PVR 14 Presentations	**14** Study ?s 13-14 Point of View	**15** Writing Assignment #3
16 Group Theme Research & Discussion	**17** Group Theme Presenations	**18** Extra Discussion ?s Preparation	**19** Extra Discussion?s Discussion	**20** Vocabulary Review
21 Unit Review	**22** Unit Test			

Key: P = Preview Study Questions V = Vocabulary Work R = Read

STUDY GUIDE QUESTIONS

STUDY GUIDE QUESTIONS *The Secret Life of Bees*

Assignment 1

Chapter 1

1. Who is Lily?
2. Who is Rosaleen?
3. Lily wakes up T. Ray in the middle of the night to show him something. What does she want to show him? Why?
4. What happened to Lily's mother?
5. What does Lily think will give her a "real chance" to learn how to be a beautiful, fashionable girl?
6. Lily captures bees and puts them in a jar to prove to T. Ray that they really do exist. How does she take care of them, and how do they fare?
7. How did Lily discover Rosaleen loved her "beyond reason"?
8. What daydreams did Lily have about Rosaleen?
9. Identify Deborah and tell three "scraps of information" Lily knows about her.
10. What items were in the paper bag Lily found in the attic?
11. What did Mrs. Henry do for Lily?
12. Before Lily went into first grade, T. Ray came to the peach stand to tell her something. What did he want to tell her? Why?
13. What major event on television captures Rosaleen's total attention?
14. When Lily asks for the silver charm bracelet for her birthday, T. Ray just looks at her and then keeps on eating. What effect does his response have on her?
15. During the overnight hours after she had asked for the charm bracelet, Lily sneaks out of the house and goes somewhere. Where does she go? Why?
16. Why does T. Ray make Lily kneel down on the Martha White grits?
17. The morning after she is punished for being in the orchard, Lily wakes up late. T. Ray yells at her for not going to work at the peach stand on time. What does Lily understand after T. Ray tells her, "As long as you're under my roof, you'll do what I say!"?
18. Why does Rosaleen want to go to town?
19. For what is Rosaleen arrested?

Assignment 2

Chapters 2-3

1. When the dealer hits Rosaleen on the head with a flashlight and Lily screams, what is Mr. Avery Gaston's response?
2. After T. Ray gets Lily out of jail, they have a fight. What does T. Ray say to Lily that "would sink [her] forever"?
3. After Lily pours the tear drop out of the bottom of the bee jar, she has a "true religious moment" and hears a voice say something. What does the voice say?
4. Where does Lily go first when she leaves home, and how does she get there?
5. Why isn't Rosaleen at the jail when Lily goes back to see her?
6. How does Lily get Rosaleen out of the hospital?

7. Where do Lily and Rosaleen go after they escape from the hospital? How do they get there?
8. After Lily and Rosaleen are dropped off outside of Tiburon, they have a fight and part ways for a short while. How and where do they get back together?
9. Lily sees something in the Frogmore Stew General Store and Restaurant that shocks her. What does she see?
10. Identify August Boatwright.

Assignment 3
Chapters 4-5

1. When Lily first arrives at the Boatwrights' house, she looks around and comes upon the black Madonna. How does the black Madonna make Lily feel?
2. When August says, "Who've we got here?" what is Lily's reply, and how does August respond to that?
3. Lily knows her mother was from Virginia and tells August that she and Rosaleen are headed to Virginia to find her aunt there. What does August say that electrifies Lily?
4. What first lets Lily know she has some prejudice buried inside herself?
5. What is odd about the stone wall Lily comes upon in the woods?
6. What does May do when an unpleasant topic is brought up? What is the only thing that seems to help her get over it?
7. How do June and August feel about Lily and Rosaleen?
8. For what special help did Lily pray to Mary?
9. Name the rules for "bee yard etiquette."
10. August tells Lily how May is special. What does she say?
11. Who was April, and what happened to her?
12. What is the "wailing wall"?
13. What does Lily do at the wailing wall?

Assignment 4
Chapters 6-7

1. When Neil appears on the scene, what does Lily learn about him and June from May?
2. Who are The Daughters of Mary?
3. Briefly re-tell the story of Our Lady of Chains.
4. What happens when Lily goes to touch the heart of Our Lady of Chains?
5. What is Lily's first impression of Zach?
6. What surprises Zach about Lily?
7. Lily tells Zach, "You've got to hear of these things before you can imagine them." What is Zach's response?
8. What feelings does Lily discover when she and Zach go into the country to harvest honey?
9. When Zach stops at a stop sign next to the Dixie Cafe, Lily declares she "will never throw rose petals to anybody." What happens next?
10. How does Lily feel about Rosaleen's moving to May's room?

11. What happens when Neil and June are picking tomatoes?

Assignment 5

Chapter 8

1. What does Lily learn from August while they are pasting labels on the jars of honey?
2. What does August say is the whole problem with people?
3. What is the relationship of the queen bee to all the other bees in the hive?
4. How does Lily feel when she and August go to collect honey, and the bees come out and fly around her?
5. What news does Zach bring on the lunch feast day?
6. Who does Lily call from Mr. Forrest's office? Why?
7. Lily writes a letter to T. Ray then tears it up. That night, what did Lily do in the parlor?

Assignment 6

Chapter 9

1. What is the result of Lily and June's fighting over the water sprinkler?
2. What does Lily say about people having steel plates in their heads?
3. What does Lily discover May doing that made her have a strange, thick feeling inside and made her feel trembly?
4. What critical piece of information does May tell Lily?
5. What happens when Zach and Lily ride to town to get a new radiator hose?
6. What happens to May when she finds out about Zach's being arrested?

Assignment 7

Chapter 10

1. What happens to May after she goes to the wailing wall for the last time?
2. What messages does Lily have for May during the vigil?
3. How does Zach get out of jail?
4. What is August's reply when Lily asks if she believes putting black cloths over the hives will help May get to heaven?
5. What brings Lily the most cause for gladness while the Daughters of Mary are holding vigil for May?
6. What important message is in May's note to August and June?
7. What is August's advice to June after reading May's note?

Assignment 8

Chapter 11

1. What is Mary Day?
2. What big event happens on the first morning of Mary Day?
3. Why does Lily leave the honey house while everyone seems to be meditating with Our Lady in Chains?
4. What promise does Zach make to Lily?

Assignment 9
Chapter 12

1. When Lily looks into the book called *Mary Through The Ages* in August's room, what most shocks her?
2. What reason does August give Lily for not telling her sooner about her mother?
3. Why did June treat Lily so badly when she first came to the Boatwrights' house?
4. Identify Tica Tee.
5. Why did Deborah Fontanel come to Sylvan?
6. Why did Deborah marry T. Ray?
7. What does August tell Lily about her mother that makes Lily say, "I hate her"?
8. What has August had to live without knowing all these years?
9. What are August's parting words to Lily as she stands in the doorway after putting her to bed on the night of their big conversation?

Assignment 10
Chapter 13

1. What does Lily do after August leaves her in the honey house after their talk?
2. What is Rosaleen's response when Lily asks her why she never told her what she knew about her mother?
3. Why do the Daughters of Mary rub honey all over Our Lady?
4. What does the hat box August brings to Lily in the honey house contain?
5. Why is the photograph in the hat box so important?

Assignment 11
Chapter 14

1. How does having her mother's things and knowing the whole story affect Lily? What does she do?
2. Where does Rosaleen go in her new red dress with big white flowers?
3. After talking with Zach on the telephone, Lily thinks, "Both of us, it seemed like, were doomed to misery." What does she mean?
4. Lily sees August and June hugging on the floor. What does August say to June that she intends also for Lily?
5. What does August take Lily out to see first thing in the morning?
6. What happens to the bees when the queen dies?
7. What does August tell Lily that she always wants Lily to remember?
8. How does T. Ray find Lily?
9. What happens in the afternoon after August had taken Lily to see the queenless colony?
10. What happens to T. Ray when he finds out that Deborah had been at the Boatwrights' home when she left him?
11. What brings T. Ray back to his senses?
12. What declaration does Lily make to T. Ray?
13. Who comes to help Lily in her struggle against T. Ray?

14. What does August do to help diffuse the situation between T. Ray and Lily?
15. Lily runs after T. Ray as he leaves, yelling for him to stop. What does she ask him, and what is his response?
16. Who is Becca?
17. What are Becca and Lily called at school? Why?
18. What is the closing image of the novel?

Assignment 1

Chapter 1

1. Who is Lily?
   Lily is the narrator of the story. She is a fourteen-year-old girl who lives with her father.
2. Who is Rosaleen?
   Rosaleen is the housekeeper and "stand-in mother" for Lily.
3. Lily wakes up T. Ray in the middle of the night to show him something. What does she want to show him? Why?
   Lily wants to show T. Ray the swarm of bees in her room. She thinks the bees are quite a spectacle and wants to share the sight with someone. T. Ray is the only person around with whom she could share it with.
4. What happened to Lily's mother?
   When she was four years old, Lily accidently shot and killed her mother.
5. What does Lily think will give her a "real chance" to learn how to be a beautiful, fashionable girl?
   She thinks charm school would teach her all the things she needs to know.
6. Lily captures bees and puts them in a jar to prove to T. Ray that they really do exist. How does she take care of them, and how do they fare?
   She is sure to leave holes in the lid for air to circulate, she puts in beautiful flowers with lots of pollen, and tries to make the jar as comfortable as possible. The bees, however, don't fare so well in captivity. They desperately try to get out, wear themselves out, and eventually give up. When the jar is opened, the bees remain there, "as if the world had shrunk to that jar."
7. How did Lily discover Rosaleen loved her "beyond reason"?
   Rosaleen allowed Lily to bring home an Easter-dyed baby chick when she was eight. When T. Ray tried to take it away, Rosaleen stood up on Lily's behalf, telling T. Ray, "You ain't touching that chick."
8. What daydreams did Lily have about Rosaleen?
   "I used to have daydreams in which she was white and married T. Ray, and became my real mother. Other times I was a Negro orphan she found in a cornfield and adopted. Once in a while I had us living in a foreign country like New York, where she could adopt me and we could both stay our natural color."
9. Identify Deborah and tell three "scraps of information" Lily knows about her.
   Deborah was Lily's mother. She was from Virginia. She was an only child whose mother has since passed away, and she was a "lunatic" when it came to saving bugs.
10. What items were in the paper bag Lily found in the attic?
    The bag contained a picture of her mother, a pair of white, cotton gloves, and a picture of a black Madonna with "Tiburon, S.C." hand written on the back.
11. What did Mrs. Henry do for Lily?
    Mrs. Henry made some comments to Lily that made her realize she was smart and had the potential for a future beyond anything she had previously imagined for herself.
12. Before Lily went into first grade, T. Ray came to the peach stand to tell her something. What did he want to tell her? Why?
    He wanted to tell her how her mother died so she wouldn't hear it from other people at school.
13. What major event on television captures Rosaleen's total attention?
    President Johnson signs the Civil Rights Act into law.

14. When Lily asks for the silver charm bracelet for her birthday, T. Ray just looks at her and then keeps on eating. What effect does his response have on her?
". . . it caused a kind of sorrow to rise in me that felt fresh and tender and had nothing, really, to do with the bracelet. I think now it was sorrow for the sound of his fork scraping the plate, the way it swelled in the distance between us, how I was not even in the room."
15. During the overnight hours after she had asked for the charm bracelet, Lily sneaks out of the house and goes somewhere. Where does she go? Why?
Lily waits "till it was late enough so I could slip out to the orchard and dig up the tin box that held my mother's things. I wanted to lie down in the orchard and let it hold me." She wants to escape T. Ray and the confines of the house and to go to a place where she can find some peace and comfort.
16. Why does T. Ray make Lily kneel down on the Martha White grits?
He thinks she has been in the orchard with a boy. Kneeling on the grits is her punishment for acting "no better than a slut."
17. The morning after she is punished for being in the orchard, Lily wakes up late. T. Ray yells at her for not going to work at the peach stand on time. What does Lily understand after T. Ray tells her, "As long as you're under my roof, you'll do what I say!"?
Lily understands that "a new rooftop would do wonders" for her. She understands that she needs to leave home.
18. Why does Rosaleen want to go to town?
She wants to register to vote.
19. For what is Rosaleen arrested?
She is arrested for assault, theft, and disturbing the peace.

Assignment 2

Chapters 2-3

1. When the dealer hits Rosaleen on the head with a flashlight and Lily screams, what is Mr. Avery Gaston's response?
He puts his hand over Lily's mouth and says, "Hush."
2. After T. Ray gets Lily out of jail, they have a fight. What does T. Ray say to Lily that "would sink [her] forever"?
He says, ". . . your sorry mother ran off and left you. The day she died, she'd come back to get her things, that's all. You can hate me all you want, but she's *the one who left you."*
3. After Lily pours the tear drop out of the bottom of the bee jar, she has a "true religious moment" and hears a voice say something. What does the voice say?
It says, "Lily Melissa Owens, your jar is open."
4. Where does Lily go first when she leaves home, and how does she get there?
She goes to the jail to see about Rosaleen. Brother Gerald picks her up along the road and takes her there.
5. Why isn't Rosaleen at the jail when Lily goes back to see her?
Mr. Gaston says Rosaleen had fallen and had been sent to the hospital for stitches and for observation because of a little concussion.
6. How does Lily get Rosaleen out of the hospital?
Lily pretends to be the jailer's wife. She telephones the nurse's station and asks the nurse to tell the policeman at Rosaleen's room that Mr. Gaston needs him back at the jail. When the policeman leaves, Lily and Rosaleen escape from the hospital.

7. Where do Lily and Rosaleen go after they escape from the hospital? How do they get there?
   Lily and Rosaleen go to Tiburon, South Carolina. A black farmer with a load of cantaloupes picks them up on his way to market and takes them within three miles of Tiburon.
8. After Lily and Rosaleen are dropped off outside of Tiburon, they have a fight and part ways for a short while. How and where do they get back together?
   Lily wakes up after dreaming the moon was falling in pieces from the sky. She searches for Rosaleen and finds her naked, bathing in the stream. Lily strips off her clothes and goes to Rosaleen. They apologize to each other. Lily holds her breath, and sinks "as far as [she] could into that shimmering, dark world."
9. Lily sees something in the Frogmore Stew General Store and Restaurant that shocks her. What does she see?
   She sees a picture of a black Madonna that is exactly the same as her mother's.
10. Identify August Boatwright.
   August is the beekeeper who makes the honey that goes into the black Madonna-labeled jars.

Assignment 3

<u>Chapters 4-5</u>

1. When Lily first arrives at the Boatwrights' house, she looks around and comes upon the black Madonna. How does the black Madonna make Lily feel?
   ". . . [she] made me feel my glory and my shame at the same time."
2. When August says, "Who've we got here?" what is Lily's reply, and how does August respond to that?
   Lily introduces herself and Rosaleen and simply tells August that they have run away from home and have no place to go. August offers to let them stay until they can figure out what to do.
3. Lily knows her mother was from Virginia and tells August that she and Rosaleen are headed to Virginia to find her aunt there. What does August say that electrifies Lily?
   August says that she is from Virginia, too.
4. What first lets Lily know she has some prejudice buried inside herself?
   ". . . all I could think was August is so intelligent, so cultured, *and I was surprised by this. That's what let me know I had some prejudice buried inside me."*
5. What is odd about the stone wall Lily comes upon in the woods?
   It has tiny pieces of folded-up paper with writing on them stuck between the stones.
6. What does May do when an unpleasant topic is brought up? What is the only thing that seems to help her get over it?
   May starts frantically singing, "Oh! Susanna." The only thing that seems to help her get over it is to "go to the wall."
7. How do June and August feel about Lily and Rosaleen?
   June doesn't want Lily and Rosaleen staying with them. She wants to send them away. August, however, wants to help them, to be patient and see why they have dropped on the Boatwrights' doorstep.
8. For what special help did Lily pray to Mary?
   ". . . I asked her to see to it that I never went back. I asked her to draw a curtain around the pink house so no one would ever find us. I asked this daily . . . . "

9. Name the rules for "bee yard etiquette."
Don't be afraid. Don't be an idiot. Don't swat. If you feel angry, whistle. Act like you know what you're doing, even if you don't. Send the bees love.

10. August tells Lily how May is special. What does she say?
". . . It's like we have built-in protection around our hearts that keeps the pain from overwhelming us. But May--she doesn't have that. Everything just comes to her--all the suffering out there--and she feels as if it's happening to her. She can't tell the difference."

11. Who was April, and what happened to her?
April was May's twin sister. She was unable to accept society's unfairness, became depressed, and killed herself at age 15.

12. What is the "wailing wall"?
It is a wall in Jerusalem where the Jewish people go to mourn. They write their prayers on scraps of paper and tuck them into the wall. June and August came up with the idea of a wailing wall to help May deal with her issues.

13. What does Lily do at the wailing wall?
She puts her mother's name on a slip of paper into the wall.

Assignment 4

Chapters 6-7

1. When Neil appears on the scene, what does Lily learn about him and June from May?
She learns that Neil wants to marry June, but she has been putting him off for a long time. June was jilted at the altar by a previous fiancee.

2. Who are The Daughters of Mary?
They are a group of women (and one man) who meet at the Boatwrights' house to honor and pray to Mary. They were Queenie, Violet, Lunelle, Mabelee, Cressie, Sugar-Girl, and Otis.

3. Briefly re-tell the story of Our Lady of Chains.
The slaves had prayed to the Lord for help. One day a slave named Obadiah found a statue of a black woman with her fist sticking up. He heard the statue say, "It's all right. I'm here. I'll be taking care of you now." She was carried to the praise house, where the slaves came to pray. They sang and prayed and came to touch her heart, and she filled their hearts with fearlessness and whispered plans of escape to them. The slaves began escaping to the north. The masters removed the statue from the praise house and chained it into the barn 50 times, but each time the statue miraculously broke the chains and reappeared in the praise house. So she became known as Our Lady of Chains--not because she wore *chains, but because she* broke *them.*

4. What happens when Lily goes to touch the heart of Our Lady of Chains?
June stops playing, Lily freezes with her arm outstretched towards Mary, realizes she is not "one of them," hears herself calling to Mary, and faints.

5. What is Lily's first impression of Zach?
She thinks he is handsome and feels that they will become friends.

6. What surprises Zach about Lily?
She is white.

7. Lily tells Zach, "You've got to hear of these things before you can imagine them." What is Zach's response?
He says, "You've gotta imagine what's never been."

8. What feelings does Lily discover when she and Zach go into the country to harvest honey?
She is surprised to discover that she is attracted to Zach. ". . . maybe desire kicked in when it pleased without noticing the rules we lived and died by."
9. When Zach stops at a stop sign next to the Dixie Cafe, Lily declares she "will never throw rose petals to anybody." What happens next?
Lily breaks down crying, and Zach comforts her.
10. How does Lily feel about Rosaleen's moving to May's room?
She feels abandoned, hurt, and lonely.
11. What happens when Neil and June are picking tomatoes?
Neil brings up the subject of marriage again. June tells him she will never get married, and they have a big fight which ends in Neil's driving off with June telling him never to come back and throwing tomatoes at his car.

Assignment 5
<u>Chapter 8</u>

1. What does Lily learn from August while they are pasting labels on the jars of honey?
She learns how and why the black Madonna came to be on the jar labels, and she learns about August's personal history--how she was from Richmond but loved to come here to her grandmother's house, and how she came to own it.
2. What does August say is the whole problem with people?
They know *what matters, but they don't* choose *it.*
3. What is the relationship of the queen bee to all the other bees in the hive?
The queen is the mother of every bee in the hive.
4. How does Lily feel when she and August go to collect honey, and the bees come out and fly around her?
"I felt like the queen's attendants were out here in a frenzy of love, caressing me in a thousand places. Look who's here, it's Lily. She is so weary and lost. Come on, bee sisters. *I was the stamen in the middle of a twirling flower. The center of all their comforting."*
5. What news does Zach bring on the lunch feast day?
Jack Palance, the movie star, is coming to town with a black woman and plans to sit with her in the white section of the movie theater.
6. Who does Lily call from Mr. Forrest's office? Why?
Lily calls T. Ray to ask him if he knows her favorite color.
7. Lily writes a letter to T. Ray then tears it up. That night, what did Lily do in the parlor?
She touched the heart of Mary, Our Lady of Chains, and prayed to her.

Assignment 6
<u>Chapter 9</u>

1. What is the result of Lily and June's fighting over the water sprinkler?
They both end up laughing, and June hugs Lily.
2. What does Lily say about people having steel plates in their heads?
"Every human being on the face of the earth has a steel plate in his head, but if you lie down now and then and get still as you can, it will slide open like elevator doors, letting in all the secret thoughts that have been standing around so patiently, pushing a button for a ride to the top. The real troubles in life happen when those hidden doors stay closed for too long."

3. What does Lily discover May doing that made her have a strange, thick feeling inside and made her feel trembly?
   May works at luring roaches out of the house with graham cracker and marshmallow crumbs, just like Lily's mother did.
4. What critical piece of information does May tell Lily?
   May tells Lily that Deborah Fontanel stayed out in the honey house and was "the sweetest thing."
5. What happens when Zach and Lily ride to town to get a new radiator hose?
   Some of Zach's friends get into an incident with white men who were waiting for Jack Palance outside the movie theater. One of the boys throws a bottle at one of the white men and gives him a bloody nose. Zach stands with the boys, and they are all arrested.
6. What happens to May when she finds out about Zach's being arrested?
   At first she seems fine, then she goes into a kind of a trance, and then she comes back but isn't at all her usual self. She insists on going to the wall by herself.

Assignment 7

Chapter 10

1. What happens to May after she goes to the wailing wall for the last time?
   She goes to the river, pulls a rock onto herself, and drowns herself in the river.
2. What messages does Lily have for May during the vigil?
   Lily says she hopes May will be happier in heaven, to tell Mary that "we're doing our best to keep her memory going," and to find her mother and let her know that Lily is away from T. Ray and "would appreciate a sign letting her know you love her."
3. How does Zach get out of jail?
   The ticket-taker at the movie theater finally comes forward to say which of the boys threw the bottle, and the charges against Zach are dropped.
4. What is August's reply when Lily asks if she believes putting black cloths over the hives will help May get to heaven?
   August says, "Putting black cloths on the hives is for us. I do it to remind us that life gives way into death, and then death turns around and gives way into life."
5. What brings Lily the most cause for gladness while the Daughters of Mary are holding vigil for May?
   Sugar-Girl makes a joke about white people, and no one there even thinks about Lily's being white. It is like she "was truly one of them."
6. What important message is in May's note to August and June?
   "It's my time to die, and it's your time to live. Don't mess it up."
7. What is August's advice to June after reading May's note?
   She told June to marry Neil.

Assignment 8

Chapter 11

1. What is Mary Day?
   On the Feast of the Assumption (Mary's feast day), the Daughters of Mary have a big (two-day) event in which they celebrate the feast day for Mary, have a special remembrance for Our Lady of Chains, and give thanks for the honey crop.
2. What big event happens on the first morning of Mary Day?
   June finally says she will marry Neil.

3. Why does Lily leave the honey house while everyone seems to be meditating with Our Lady in Chains?
   She can't stand to see Mary wrapped in chains, and she doesn't want to meditate or remember the past.
4. What promise does Zach make to Lily?
   He says, ". . . one day, after I've gone away and become somebody, I'm gonna find you, and we'll be together then."

Assignment 9
<u>Chapter 12</u>

1. When Lily looks into the book called *Mary Through The Ages* in August's room, what most shocks her?
   In every picture where the angel Gabriel comes to tell her she is going to have "the baby of babies," he has a big white lily for her.
2. What reason does August give Lily for not telling her sooner about her mother?
   "Because you weren't ready to know about her. I didn't want to risk you running away again . . . . There's a fullness of time for things, Lily. You have to know when to prod and when to be quiet, when to let things take their course. That's what I've been trying to do."
3. Why did June treat Lily so badly when she first came to the Boatwrights' house?
   June resented Lily's mother because August had gone to work at Lily's mother's house. She took her resentment out on Deborah and on Lily.
4. Identify Tica Tee.
   Tica Tee was Lily's mother's imaginary friend.
5. Why did Deborah Fontanel come to Sylvan?
   Her mother died, leaving her alone. A friend of hers had recently moved to Sylvan and recommended it to her--and Deborah knew Sylvan was near August. Mostly she wanted to be near August.
6. Why did Deborah marry T. Ray?
   She was pregnant with Lily.
7. What does August tell Lily about her mother that makes Lily say, "I hate her"?
   August tells Lily that Deborah had come to Tiburon by herself; she had left Lily with T. Ray.
8. What has August had to live without knowing all these years?
   She never knew exactly how Deborah died.
9. What are August's parting words to Lily as she stands in the doorway after putting her to bed on the night of their big conversation?
   She says, "There is nothing perfect. There is only life."

Assignment 10
<u>Chapter 13</u>

1. What does Lily do after August leaves her in the honey house after their talk?
   She can't sleep, becomes angrier, gets up and smashes up the contents of the honey house. Then, she sits down in front of the black Madonna, drained, and falls asleep.
2. What is Rosaleen's response when Lily asks her why she never told her what she knew about her mother?
   Rosaleen says, "Oh, Lily. Why would I go and hurt you with something like that?"

3. Why do the Daughters of Mary rub honey all over Our Lady?
August said, "The churches used to bathe their special statues in holy water as a way to honor them, especially statues of Our Lady . . . . We settled on honey . . . . honey is a preservative . . . . When we bathe Our Lady in it, I guess you'd say we're preserving her for another year . . . ."
4. What does the hat box August brings to Lily in the honey house contain?
It has the things Lily's mother left when she went back to get Lily: a pocket mirror, a brush with a hair still in it, a gold whale-shaped pin, a book of English poetry August had given her, and a small oval picture frame with a picture of Deborah and Lily.
5. Why is the photograph in the hat box so important?
It shows Lily that her mother loved her. It was the sign she had been hoping for.

Assignment 11

<u>Chapter 14</u>

1. How does having her mother's things and knowing the whole story affect Lily? What does she do?
Lily pulls away into herself, wanting to be alone. She spends a period of time thinking, trying not to think, and grieving.
2. Where does Rosaleen go in her new red dress with big white flowers?
She goes to register to vote.
3. After talking with Zach on the telephone, Lily thinks, "Both of us, it seemed like, were doomed to misery." What does she mean?
She thinks she is doomed to go back to living with T. Ray, which would make her miserable, and Zach is going to a white high school, where he would be made miserable by prejudiced white people.
4. Lily sees August and June hugging on the floor. What does August say to June that she intends also for Lily?
August says, "Regrets don't help anything, you know that."
5. What does August take Lily out to see first thing in the morning?
August takes Lily to see a queenless colony of bees.
6. What happens to the bees when the queen dies?
They have no direction . . . they begin "looking melancholy . . . loafing . . . and lamenting."
7. What does August tell Lily that she always wants Lily to remember?
She says, "Our Lady is not some magical being out there somewhere, like a fairy godmother. She's not the statue in the parlor. She's something inside *you . . . . You have to find a mother inside of yourself . . . . She's the power inside you . . . . not only the power inside you but the love. And when you get down to it, Lily, that's the only purpose grand enough for a human life. Not just to love--but to* persist *in love . . . . This Mary I'm talking about sits in your heart all day long, saying, 'Lily, you are my everlasting home. Don't you ever be afraid. I am enough. We are enough.'"*
8. How does T. Ray find Lily?
His phone bill had a collect call from Mr. Clayton Forrest's office. He goes to the office and finds out from the secretary where to find Lily.
9. What happens in the afternoon after August had taken Lily to see the queenless colony?
T. Ray comes to the Boatwrights' house to take Lily home.

10. What happens to T. Ray when he finds out that Deborah had been at the Boatwrights' home when she left him?
T. Ray loses himself for a bit and confuses Lily with Deborah. He hits her and tells her she would never leave him again. He threatens her with a knife.

11. What brings T. Ray back to his senses?
Lily yells at him, "Daddy!"

12. What declaration does Lily make to T. Ray?
She tells him she will not go back with him.

13. Who comes to help Lily in her struggle against T. Ray?
August and Rosaleen are the first to arrive, but Lily waves them off. Then, the other available Daughters of Mary arrive, prepared to fight for Lily.

14. What does August do to help diffuse the situation between T. Ray and Lily?
She says that T. Ray would be doing them all a favor by letting Lily stay, and she promises to take good care of Lily and keep her straight. She gives him a way out of the situation.

15. Lily runs after T. Ray as he leaves, yelling for him to stop. What does she ask him, and what is his response?
Lily asks him for the truth about her mother's death, if she really did accidentally kill her mother. T. Ray softens and confesses that she really did do it without meaning to.

16. Who is Becca?
Becca is Clayton Forrest's daughter who sometimes comes by to visit with Lily.

17. What are Becca and Lily called at school? Why?
They are called "nigger lovers" because they associate with Zach at school.

18. What is the closing image of the novel?
The women in Lily's life are standing strongly behind her--her mothers.

MULTIPLE CHOICE STUDY/QUIZ QUESTIONS

The Secret Life of Bees

Assignment 1
Chapter 1

1. Identify Lily.
   - A. The narrator catches a bee in a mason jar and names it Lily.
   - B. Lily is the narrator's mother.
   - C. Lily is the narrator's nanny and housekeeper.
   - D. Lily is the narrator of the story. She is a fourteen-year-old girl who lives with her father.

2. Who is Rosaleen?
   - A. Rosaleen is the name of T. Ray's truck.
   - B. Rosaleen is the narrator.
   - C. Rosaleen is the narrator's mother.
   - D. Rosaleen is the housekeeper and "stand-in mother" for Lily.

3. Lily wakes up T. Ray in the middle of the night to show him something. What does she want to show him?
   - A. Lily wants to show T. Ray the swarm of bees in her room.
   - B. Lily wants to show T. Ray a poem she wrote.
   - C. Lily wants to show T. Ray some things she found in the attic.
   - D. Lily wants to show T. Ray that a bee has stung her.

4. What happened to Lily's mother?
   - A. Lily's mother was killed in an automobile accident by a drunk driver.
   - B. When she was four years old, Lily accidently shot and killed her mother.
   - C. Lily's mother left and never returned; no one knows exactly what happened to her.
   - D. T. Ray lost his temper and killed Lily's mother during an argument.

5. What does Lily think will give her a "real chance" to learn how to be a beautiful, fashionable girl?
   - A. A new mother
   - B. A fashion magazine subscription
   - C. Charm school
   - D. A new television show

6. Lily captures bees and puts them in a jar to prove to T. Ray that they really do exist. Which of the following statements about how she takes care of them and how they fare is NOT true?
   A. The bees desperately try to get out, wear themselves out, and eventually give up.
   B. She leaves holes in the lid for air to circulate.
   C. She puts beautiful flowers with lots of pollen in the jar.
   D. She puts a little tin of water in the jar for the bees.

7. How did Lily discover Rosaleen loved her "beyond reason"?
   A. Rosaleen told T. Ray, "I'll gather them bees up and put 'em in your bed if I sees you hit that girl again."
   B. Rosaleen told T. Ray, "Don't you blame Lily for what you done to your own wife!"
   C. Rosaleen told T. Ray, "You ain't touching that chick."
   D. Rosaleen told T. Ray, "No more Martha Whites!"

8. Which statement does NOT describe daydreams Lily had about Rosaleen?
   A. I sometimes dreamed that she would get a new job with a rich family, and T. Ray would be put in jail for his meanness. The rich family would adopt me, and I could live with Rosaleen forever.
   B. I dreamed we were in a foreign country like New York, where she could adopt me and we could both stay our natural color.
   C. I dreamed I was a Negro orphan she found in a cornfield and adopted.
   D. I used to have daydreams in which she was white and married T. Ray, and became my real mother.

9. Which is NOT a "scrap of information" Lily knows about her mother?
   A. She was from Virginia.
   B. She used to be a waitress.
   C. She was a lunatic when it came to saving bugs.
   D. She was an only child.

10. Which item was NOT in the paper bag Lily found in the attic?
   A. A picture of Lily's mother
   B. A picture of a black Madonna
   C. A brush with a few strands of long, blonde hair
   D. A pair of white, cotton gloves

11. What did Mrs. Henry do for Lily?
   A. She bought extra peaches from Lily.
   B. She suggested good books for Lily to read.
   C. She helped Lily realize she was smart.
   D. She gave Lily fashion magazines.

12. Before Lily went into first grade, T. Ray came to the peach stand to tell her something. What did he want to tell her?
   A. He wanted to tell her he loved her.
   B. He wanted to tell her about his past.
   C. He wanted to tell her how her mother died.
   D. He wanted to tell her about her grandmother.

13. What major event on television captures Rosaleen's total attention?
   A. President Johnson signing the Civil Rights Act into law
   B. The first moon landing
   C. President Kennedy's assassination
   D. Martin Luther King, Jr.'s speech

14. When Lily asks for the silver charm bracelet for her birthday, T. Ray just looks at her and then keeps on eating. What effect does his response have on her?
   A. ". . . it burst any bubble of hope I had . . . ."
   B. ". . . it seemed funny to me . . . ."
   C. ". . . it caused a kind of sorrow to rise in me . . . ."
   D. ". . . it caused anger to rise in me . . . ."

15. During the overnight hours after she had asked for the charm bracelet, Lily sneaks out of the house and goes somewhere. Where does she go?
   A. T. Ray's room
   B. Rosaleen's room
   C. The orchard
   D. The kitchen

16. Why does T. Ray make Lily kneel down on the Martha White grits?
   A. He thinks she has become too sassy.
   B. He thinks she needs to learn self-discipline.
   C. He thinks she has been in the orchard with a boy.
   D. He thinks capturing the bees is cruel.

17. The morning after she is punished for being in the orchard, Lily wakes up late. T. Ray yells at her for not going to work at the peach stand on time. What does Lily understand after T. Ray tells her, "As long as you're under my roof, you'll do what I say!"?

   A. She understands that T. Ray is a tyrant.
   B. She understands why her mother left.
   C. She understands that she needs to leave home.
   D. She understands that T. Ray loves her.

18. Why does Rosaleen want to go to town?

   A. She wants to get her hair done.
   B. She wants to register to vote.
   C. She wants to see what is going on there.
   D. She wants to buy a birthday present for Lily.

19. Which of the following is NOT something for which Rosaleen is arrested?

   A. Theft
   B. Assault
   C. Disturbing the Peace
   D. Grand Larceny

Assignment 2
Chapters 2-3

1. When the dealer hits Rosaleen on the head with a flashlight and Lily screams, what is Mr. Avery Gaston's response?
   A. He immediately attacks and apprehends the dealer.
   B. He says, "Serves you right you crazy old woman!"
   C. He shouts, "Stop! What do you think you're doing?"
   D. He puts his hand over Lily's mouth and says, "Hush."

2. After T. Ray gets Lily out of jail, they have a fight. What does T. Ray say to Lily that "would sink [her] forever"?
   A. He says, ". . . your sorry mother ran off and left you."
   B. He says, ". . . your mother was a cowardly slut."
   C. He says, ". . . you ain't nothin' but a yoke around my neck!"
   D. He says, ". . . I never wanted you."

3. After Lily pours the tear drop out of the bottom of the bee jar, she has a "true religious moment" and hears a voice say something. What does the voice say?
   A. It says, "Lily Melissa Owens, your jar is open."
   B. It says, "Lily Melissa Owens, pray for forgiveness."
   C. It says, "Lily Melissa Owens, it's now or never."
   D. It says, "Lily Melissa Owens, that man is holding you back."

4. Where does Lily go first when she leaves home, and how does she get there?
   A. She goes to town to catch a bus. Rosaleen takes her there.
   B. She goes to see Mrs. Henry. She drives the farm truck.
   C. She goes to the jail to see about Rosaleen. Brother Gerald picks her up along the road and takes her there.
   D. She goes to talk to Brother Gerald at the church. She walks there.

5. Why isn't Rosaleen at the jail when Lily goes back to see her?
   A. She had been sent to the hospital.
   B. She had been transferred.
   C. She had gone home.
   D. She had been released.

6. How does Lily get Rosaleen out of the hospital?
   A. She sneaks Rosaleen past the guard while he is sleeping.
   B. She wheels Rosaleen right out the front door in a wheel chair.
   C. She tricks the guard into leaving.
   D. She causes a diversion down the hall.

7. Where do Lily and Rosaleen go after they escape from the hospital? How do they get there?
   A. They ride in a farm wagon to South Carolina.
   B. They hitchhike to Tiburon.
   C. They get a ride in a farm truck and sneak back to the house to collect a few of Rosaleen's things.
   D. They take a bus to Virginia.

8. After Lily and Rosaleen are dropped off outside of Tiburon, they have a fight and part ways for a short while. Where do they get back together?
   A. Alongside the road
   B. In a stream
   C. In the woods
   D. In a boat

9. Lily sees something in the Frogmore Stew General Store and Restaurant that shocks her. What does she see?
   A. She sees a woman who looks exactly like her mother.
   B. She sees T. Ray.
   C. She sees a poster with pictures of her and Rosaleen on it.
   D. She sees a picture of a black Madonna that is exactly the same as her mother's.

10. Identify August Boatwright.
   A. August is the beekeeper who makes the honey that goes into the black Madonna-labeled jars.
   B. August is Rosaleen's sister.
   C. August answers the door on that first day. She plays the cello and is rather unfriendly.
   D. August is the storekeeper at the Frogmore Stew General Store and Restaurant.

Assignment 3
Chapters 4-5

1. When Lily first arrives at the Boatwrights' house, she looks around and comes upon the black Madonna. How does the black Madonna make Lily feel?
   A. ". . . [she] made me feel my glory and my shame at the same time."
   B. ". . . [she] made me feel an uneasy hope, teasing me with possibilities."
   C. ". . . [she] made me feel all shivery, and the hairs stood up on the back of my neck."
   D. ". . . [she] made me feel a warmth and happiness I had never experienced before."

2. What is August's response when Lily tells her she and Rosaleen have run away and have no place to go?
   A. August asks if the law is after them.
   B. August offers to let them stay until they can figure out what to do.
   C. August confers with her two sisters.
   D. August makes Lily and Rosaleen feel small and degraded but agrees to let them stay.

3. Lily tells August that she and Rosaleen are headed to Virginia to find her aunt there. What does August say that electrifies Lily?
   A. August says that she is from Virginia, too.
   B. August says that there is no need for them to go on to Virginia; they may stay with her and her sisters as long as they want.
   C. August whispers to Lily that she knows a secret, back-roads route to Virginia.
   D. August tells Lily the police will probably find them before they make it to Virginia.

4. What first lets Lily know she has some prejudice buried inside herself?
   A. She is surprised that the food at dinner is just ordinary food.
   B. She is surprised that the sisters keep such a neat, clean house.
   C. She is surprised that the sisters speak so well.
   D. She is surprised that August is so cultured and intelligent.

5. What is odd about the stone wall Lily comes upon in the woods?
   A. It has been painted the color of honey.
   B. It has tiny pieces of folded-up paper with writing on them stuck between the stones.
   C. It is made of both stone and small tree branches.
   D. It seems to loop in a circle.

6. What does May do when an unpleasant topic is brought up?
   A. May changes the topic immediately.
   B. May begins laughing hysterically.
   C. May runs from the room.
   D. May starts frantically singing, "Oh! Susanna."

7. How do June and August feel about Lily and Rosaleen?
   A. August does not want the visitors to stay; June does.
   B. June does not want the visitors to stay; August does.
   C. Neither August nor June wants the visitors to stay.
   D. Both August and June want the visitors to stay.

8. For what special help did Lily pray to Mary?
   A. ". . . I asked her to draw a curtain around the pink house so no one would ever find us. I asked this daily. . . . "
   B. ". . . I asked her to make August like me and want to keep me. I asked this daily. . . . "
   C. ". . . I asked her to forgive me. I asked this daily. . . . "
   D. ". . . I asked her to help T. Ray learn to be less mean and more forgiving. I asked this daily. . . . "

9. Which is NOT one of the rules for "bee yard etiquette"?
   A. Don't be afraid.
   B. Don't shake the smoker.
   C. Don't swat.
   D. Send the bees love.

10. August tells Lily how May is special. What does she say?
   A. May was injured at birth and has never had a normal mental capacity.
   B. May was born in Mary's month, making her the most special of the sisters.
   C. May feels as if all the suffering in the world is actually happening to her.
   D. May has a gift for relieving others' pain and taking it onto herself.

11. Who was April, and what happened to her?

A. April was May's twin sister who killed herself at age 15.

B. April was the Boatwright sister who had been found beaten to death in the woods.

C. April was the oldest of the Boatright sisters who got married and lived in Virginia.

D. April was the youngest of the Boatwright sisters who was drowned in an accident on the river.

12. Which statement is NOT true about the "wailing wall"?

A. May writes her troubles on scraps of paper and tucks them into the wall.

B. It runs all the way to the river.

C. May builds onto the wall.

D. June and August came up with the idea of a wailing wall to help May deal with her issues.

13. What is on the slip of paper Lily puts into the wailing wall?

A. Her mother's name

B. T. Ray's name

C. Rosaleen's name

D. Her own name

Assignment 4
Chapters 6-7

1. When Neil appears on the scene, what does Lily learn about him and June from May?
    A. She learns that Neil and June met six years ago at a symphonic performance at the college, and they have been sweethearts ever since.
    B. She learns that Neil and June have been best friends for over twenty years.
    C. She learns that Neil wants to marry June, but she has been putting him off for a long time.
    D. She learns that June really wants to marry Neil, but Neil isn't ready to settle down yet.

2. Who are The Daughters of Mary?
    A. They are a group of women (and one man) who meet at the Boatwrights' house to honor and pray to Mary, the mother of Jesus.
    B. They are Queenie, Sugar, Neil, and the Boatwright sisters.
    C. They are a group of friends who get together every week just to chat and have fun.
    D. They are a group of black women devoted to Civil Rights and Women's Rights.

3. Which of the statements below is NOT a part of the story of Our Lady of Chains?
    A. The statue was named Our Lady of Chains because she wore the chains the masters placed on her.
    B. A slave named Obadiah found a statue of a black woman with her fist sticking up.
    C. The statue said, "It's all right. I'm here. I'll be taking care of you now."
    D. The masters removed the statue from the praise house and chained it into the barn 50 times, but each time the statue miraculously broke the chains and reappeared in the praise house.

4. Which of these events does NOT happen when Lily goes to touch the heart of Our Lady of Chains?
    A. The Daughters of Mary collectively and spontaneously gasp.
    B. Lily faints.
    C. Lily freezes with her arm outstretched towards Mary.
    D. June stops playing music.

5. What is Lily's first impression of Zach?
    A. She is impressed by his physique but is afraid of him.
    B. She thinks he is handsome and feels that they will become friends.
    C. He reminds her of T. Ray in some ways.
    D. She isn't sure whether or not to trust him.

6. What surprises Zach about Lily?
   A. She looks so much like her mother.
   B. She is younger than he thought.
   C. She is older than he thought.
   D. She is white.

7. Lily tells Zach, "You've got to hear of these things before you can imagine them." What is Zach's response?
   A. He says, "Not me."
   B. He says, "Hearing things isn't everything."
   C. He says, "You've gotta imagine what's never been."
   D. He says, "Imagination is God's greatest gift to man."

8. What does Lily discover when she and Zach go into the country to harvest honey?
   A. She discovers that she is attracted to Zach.
   B. She discovers she is more prejudiced than she thought.
   C. She discovers how smart Zach is.
   D. She discovers she has a real knack for harvesting honey.

9. When Zach stops at a stop sign next to the Dixie Cafe, Lily declares she "will never throw rose petals to anybody." What happens next?
   A. A white man throws a beer bottle at their car, changing the mood completely.
   B. Zach tells her to get out of the truck.
   C. Lily breaks down crying, and Zach comforts her.
   D. They go into the cafe to eat lunch, and Zach buys roses for Lily.

10. How does Lily feel about Rosaleen's moving to May's room?
   A. She is jealous of May.
   B. She feels abandoned, hurt, and lonely.
   C. She doesn't really care that Rosaleen is moving.
   D. She is glad to finally have the room all to herself.

11. What happens when Neil and June are picking tomatoes?
   A. Neil and June have a long talk, and Neil promises never to bring up the subject of marriage again.
   B. June is bitten by a snake.
   C. They get into a fight, and June throws tomatoes at his truck as he leaves.
   D. Neil again asks June to marry him, and she finally accepts.

Assignment 5
Chapter 8

1. Which of the statements below is NOT something Lily learns from August while they are pasting labels on the jars of honey?
   A. She learns that August lived in Richmond but came here to visit her grandmother.
   B. She learns that August was once married, but her husband died.
   C. She learns how August came to own the house and bee business.
   D. She learns how and why the black Madonna came to be on the jar labels.

2. What does August say is the whole problem with people?
   A. They *think* they are doing good things, but what they choose to do is usually *not* good.
   B. They are too stupid to see just how prejudiced they are.
   C. They *know* what matters, but they don't *choose* it.
   D. People are too blinded by their own prejudices to choose wisely.

3. What is the relationship of the queen bee to all the other bees in the hive?
   A. The queen is the mother of every bee in the hive.
   B. The queen is the provider for every bee in the hive.
   C. The queen is the mate of every bee in the hive.
   D. The queen is the guardian of every bee in the hive.

4. How does Lily feel when she and August go to collect honey, and the bees come out and fly around her?
   A. She feels like she is the center of all their comforting.
   B. The bees remind her of a posse, and she thinks about T. Ray and the police coming after her.
   C. She feels like she is part of the swarm . . . a bee, carefree and secure for the first time in her life.
   D. She feels like she is the object of their attack.

5. What news does Zach bring on the lunch feast day?
   A. A white man took a black woman to the movie theater and they tried to sit in the white section, causing a small riot.
   B. A movie about a white man and a black woman is coming to the movie theater in a couple of weeks, and it is causing quite a stir in town.
   C. A white movie star is coming to town with a black woman and plans to sit with her in the white section of the movie theater.
   D. There is a movie playing at the movie theater about a white man and a black woman.

6. Who does Lily call from Mr. Forrest's office?
   A. Lily calls T. Ray.
   B. Lily calls Rosaleen.
   C. Lily calls Neil.
   D. Lily calls August.

7. Lily writes a letter to T. Ray then tears it up. That night, what does Lily do in the parlor?
   A. She cries herself to sleep in the parlor.
   B. She writes a letter to Zach instead.
   C. She burns the letter scraps in front of Mary, Our Lady of Chains.
   D. She touches the heart of Mary, Our Lady of Chains, and prays to her.

Assignment 6
Chapter 9

1. What is the result of Lily and June's fighting over the water sprinkler?
   A. Lily gets a bad cut over her left eye, which has to be bandaged.
   B. Lily's face gets covered in mud, and June makes a curt, racial remark.
   C. They both end up laughing, and June hugs Lily.
   D. June falls down in the slippery grass, and Lily laughs at her.

2. What does Lily say people have in their heads?
   A. Bees
   B. Too many wrong ideas
   C. Cobwebs
   D. Steel plates

3. What does Lily discover May doing that made her have a strange, thick feeling inside and made her feel trembly?
   A. May is luring roaches out of the house with graham cracker and marshmallow crumbs.
   B. May is putting a letter addressed to T. Ray into the mailbox.
   C. May is conversing with an imaginary companion named Deborah.
   D. May is writing Lily's name on a paper to go into the wall.

4. What critical piece of information does May tell Lily?
   A. May tells Lily that she worked for T. Ray's family when T. Ray was a young boy.
   B. May tells Lily that August is actually Lily's grandmother.
   C. May tells Lily that Deborah Fontanel stayed out in the honey house.
   D. May tells Lily that Zach loves Lily.

5. What happens when Zach and Lily ride to town to get a new radiator hose?
   A. Zach gets Jack Palance's autograph.
   B. Zach kisses Lily.
   C. Zach is arrested.
   D. Some white men beat up Zach.

6. What sets off May just before she insists on going to the wall by herself?
   A. She learns that Lily is Deborah's daughter.
   B. She learns that Zach has been arrested.
   C. Rosaleen tells May the truth about herself and Lily.
   D. She learns that Dr. Martin Luther King, Jr. has been killed.

Assignment 7
Chapter 10

1. What happens to May after she goes to the wailing wall for the last time?
   A. She aimlessly wanders into the river and drowns.
   B. She drowns herself in the river.
   C. She falls into the river and drowns.
   D. She suffocates herself under some rocks.

2. Which of the following is NOT a message Lily has for May during the vigil?
   A. Lily hopes May will be happier in heaven.
   B. Lily wants May to explain to God that Lily "just can't go back to T. Ray and will do whatever He wants if He could just keep her from being sent back."
   C. Lily wants May to tell Mary that "we're doing our best to keep her memory going."
   D. Lily wants May to find her mother and tell her Lily "would appreciate a sign letting her know you love her."

3. How does Zach get out of jail?
   A. Zach's friends feel guilty about his arrest and decide to tell the truth about who actually threw the bottle.
   B. Clayton Forrest gets him released.
   C. Zach convinces Mr. Hazelwurst that he could not have been the one who threw the bottle. Mr. Hazelwurst believed him and let him go.
   D. The charges are dropped when the ticket-taker at the movie theater identifies the real culprit.

4. What is August's reply when Lily asks if she believes putting black cloths over the hives will help May get to heaven?
   A. August says, "Putting black cloths on the hives is for us. I do it to remind us that life gives way into death, and then death turns around and gives way into life."
   B. August smiles and says, "No, child, I know May has already gone to heaven. The bees know when we're upset, though, and they get upset, too. Covering the hives helps to keep them calmer and happier."
   C. August says, "No, I don't. But I do believe in tradition, that traditions help us get through times like these. So I put on the cloths."
   D. August says, "It isn't that the hives are covered, it's the covering of the hives that helps--helps us, not May. Keeping busy distracts us a little and gives us time to accept the loss without being totally focussed on it."

5. What brings Lily the most cause for gladness while the Daughters of Mary are holding vigil for May?
   A. Sugar-Girl makes a joke about white people, and no one there even thinks about Lily's being white. It was like she was truly one of them.
   B. Rosaleen makes Lily's favorite little cakes, the ones she has loved since she was little.
   C. June and August come sit next to her, one on either side, and August puts her arm around Lily.
   D. Zach is released from jail. He comes to the house and sits vigil with Lily and the calendar sisters.

6. What important message is in May's note to August and June?
   A. "This is nobody's fault. It just is. I no longer need a wailing wall."
   B. "I don't want to be a burden to you anymore. The world is too sad of a place for me to be. Be glad I have gone on."
   C. "Our Lady of Chains told me this is the best thing for me. I have faith."
   D. "It's my time to die, and it's your time to live. Don't mess it up."

7. What does August say to June after reading May's note?
   A. She tells June to come pray with her by Our Lady of Chains.
   B. She asks June to come help her take the papers out of the wailing wall, to let them blow away in the wind.
   C. She reassures June that May has certainly gone on to heaven and tells her to be glad.
   D. She tells June to marry Neil.

Assignment 8
Chapter 11

1. Which of the following is NOT true of Mary Day?
   - A. It is the Feast of the Assumption (Mary's feast day).
   - B. It is a time to "give up" something in honor of Mary.
   - C. It is a big, two-day event in special remembrance of Mary.
   - D. It is a time to give thanks for the honey crop.

2. What big event happens on the first morning of Mary Day?
   - A. The police come to inquire about Rosaleen.
   - B. June finally says she will marry Neil.
   - C. Lily has her talk with August.
   - D. T. Ray shows up to get Lily.

3. Which is NOT a reason Lily leaves the honey house while everyone seems to be meditating with Our Lady of Chains?
   - A. She can't stand to see Mary wrapped in chains.
   - B. She doesn't want to meditate.
   - C. She doesn't want to remember the past.
   - D. She feels like she is about to faint and needs fresh air.

4. What promise does Zach make to Lily?
   - A. He says, ". . . just like the honey bee returns home to the hive, I'll come back to you."
   - B. He says, ". . . one day, after I've gone away and become somebody, I'm gonna find you, and we'll be together then."
   - C. He says, ". . . and there will come a time when the world will understand that, black or white, we are all human with human hearts and desires. You will always be in my heart, always be my true love, always be my best friend."
   - D. He says, ". . . and I won't ever let them make you go back to T. Ray."

Assignment 9
Chapter 12

1. When Lily looks into the book called *Mary Through The Ages* in August's room, what most shocks her?
   A. The text is written in Latin, and the pictures appear to be hand-painted, not reproductions.
   B. In every picture where the angel Gabriel comes to Mary, he has a big white lily for her.
   C. In every picture Mary is black. All the angels are black. In fact, everyone in all the pictures is black.
   D. There is an inscription inside the front cover that says, "To my 'Aunt' August, With Love, Deborah."

2. What reason does August give Lily for not telling her sooner about her mother?
   A. August says she hasn't told Lily before because Lily wasn't ready to hear it.
   B. August says she hasn't told Lily before because there has been so much going on with Zach's going to jail, May's death, and the Mary Day celebrations.
   C. August says she hasn't told Lily because she and June decided it would be best to wait.
   D. August says she hasn't told Lily because she didn't realize it until just the day before.

3. Why did June treat Lily so badly when she first came to the Boatwrights' house?
   A. June was trying to protect May. She thought Lily and Rosaleen would only bring trouble and upset May.
   B. June resented Lily's mother because August had gone to work at Lily's mother's house. She took her resentment out on Deborah and on Lily.
   C. June was perfectly happy with the life she had with her sisters, without any outside interference. She resented Lily's intrusion into her life.
   D. June was afraid of having strangers in the house, not knowing what they had done or why they were running away. She didn't want any involvement with the police or any trouble.

4. Identify Tica Tee.
   A. Tica Tee is Sugar-Girl's daughter.
   B. Tica Tee was Deborah's nickname for August.
   C. Tica Tee was Lily's mother's imaginary friend.
   D. Tica Tee was Lily's mother's favorite doll.

5. Why did Deborah Fontanel come to Sylvan?

   A. She was going to school there until she met T. Ray, dropped out of school, and got married.
   B. Her mother died, leaving her alone, and she wanted to be near August.
   C. A friend encouraged her to come. Her parents agreed to let her go since they knew August would be nearby in case a problem would arise.
   D. She married T. Ray, and he brought her to his home in Sylvan.

6. Why did Deborah marry T. Ray?

   A. She was drunk the night they ran off and got married.
   B. She was pregnant with Lily.
   C. She loved him.
   D. She was out of money and saw marriage as a way to survive.

7. What does August tell Lily about her mother that makes Lily say, "I hate her"?

   A. August tells Lily that Deborah had tried to commit suicide when she found out that she was pregnant.
   B. August tells Lily that Deborah came to Tiburon by herself; she had left Lily with T. Ray.
   C. August tells Lily that Deborah was a beautiful little girl with everything a little girl could want.
   D. August tells Lily that Deborah had gone to charm school and graduated at the top of her class.

8. What has August had to live without knowing all these years?

   A. She never knew exactly how Deborah died.
   B. She never knew whether or not Deborah had the child.
   C. She never knew where Deborah went or what happened to her; she just vanished.
   D. She never knew why Deborah never came back to visit.

9. What are August's parting words to Lily as she stands in the doorway after putting her to bed on the night of their big conversation?

   A. She says, "If T. Ray comes, we'll have no choice."
   B. She says, "Your mother certainly forgives you, but you will never be happy until you forgive yourself."
   C. She says, "Sleep well, Daughter of Mary."
   D. She says, "There is nothing perfect. There is only life."

Assignment 10
Chapter 13

1. What does Lily do after August leaves her in the honey house after their talk?
   A. She writes a letter to her mother.
   B. She sneaks back into the parlor to sit and talk with Our Lady of Chains.
   C. She pulls out the box with her mother's gloves and cries herself to sleep.
   D. She smashes up the contents of the honey house.

2. What is Rosaleen's response when Lily asks her why she never told her what she knew about her mother?
   A. Rosaleen says, "I didn't understand what it meant."
   B. Rosaleen says, "T. Ray told me if I ever said anything to you, he would see I got what was comin' to me."
   C. Rosaleen says, "Oh, Lily. Why would I go and hurt you with something like that?"
   D. Rosaleen says, "You didn't need to know it then."

3. Why do the Daughters of Mary rub honey all over Our Lady?
   A. As an offering for the next bee harvest
   B. To keep her color black
   C. To symbolize their sins sticking to her
   D. To preserve her

4. What does the hat box August brings to Lily in the honey house contain?
   A. It has letters Lily's mother wrote to August and a photograph.
   B. It has the things Lily's mother left when she went back to get Lily.
   C. It has the hat Lunelle made for Lily.
   D. It has a candle, beeswax, and a special seal of the black Madonna.

5. Why is the photograph in the hat box so important?
   A. The look on her mother's face shows Lily that her mother loved her.
   B. On the back it says, "My Lovely Lily" in Deborah's own handwriting, a name of endearment proving Lily's mother loved her.
   C. It is the only picture of Lily's mother and grandmother together.
   D. It shows Deborah and T. Ray, happy on their wedding day, proving that Deborah and T. Ray really were happy together at least at first.

Assignment 11
Chapter 14

1. How does having her mother's things and knowing the whole story affect Lily? What does she do?
   A. Lily's mind is finally at rest; she is happy and carefree at last.
   B. Lily has never been happier. She asks August if they can have a Deborah Day to celebrate her mother's life.
   C. Lily pulls away into herself, wanting to be alone.
   D. Lily feels the need to confront T. Ray, and she asks August if she would drive her to see him.

2. Where does Rosaleen go in her new red dress with big white flowers?
   A. She goes to register to vote.
   B. She goes shopping.
   C. She goes to church.
   D. She goes to the movies.

3. After talking with Zach on the telephone, Lily thought, *Both of us, it seemed like, were* _____.
   A. Victims of life
   B. The luckiest people alive
   C. Peas in a pod
   D. Doomed to misery

4. Lily sees August and June hugging on the floor. What does August say to June that she intended also for Lily?
   A. August says, "Never look back; the future is bright."
   B. August says, "Regrets don't help anything, you know that."
   C. August says, "Hope springs eternal."
   D. August says, "All's well that ends well."

5. Who or what does August take Lily out to see first thing in the morning?
   A. August takes Lily to see a present she has bought for Lily.
   B. August takes Lily to see the largest hive in the county.
   C. August takes Lily to see T. Ray.
   D. August takes Lily to see a queenless colony of bees.

6. What happens to the bees when the queen dies?
   A. They seal the beehive with the queen inside, and they fly off in search of a new queen.
   B. They all die.
   C. They organize themselves and go in search of a new queen.
   D. They begin looking melancholy . . . loafing . . . and lamenting.

7. What does August tell Lily that she always wants Lily to remember?
   A. She says, "Never forget Our Lady."
   B. She says, "Our Lady is taking care of your mother--and May--and she is waiting, in time, to take care of you."
   C. She says, "Our Lady is . . . something *inside* you. "
   D. She says, "You will always have a friend in me--and in Our Lady. She will always give you strength when you are in need, and I shall be here for you as long as I live."

8. How does T. Ray find Lily?
   A. August called him to tell him Lily was safe with her.
   B. May had mailed him a letter.
   C. His phone bill had a collect call from Mr. Clayton Forrest's office. He goes to the office and finds out from the secretary where to find Lily.
   D. He goes snooping around town asking questions, and someone remembered seeing her with Zach on the day he was arrested. He followed that lead to the Boatwrights' house.

9. What happens in the afternoon after August had taken Lily to see the queenless colony?
   A. June and Neil get married.
   B. T. Ray comes to the Boatwrights' house to take Lily home.
   C. The Daughters of Mary come for their weekly meeting.
   D. Our Lady of Chains goes missing.

10. Which of the following did NOT happen when T. Ray found out that Deborah had been at the Boatwrights' when she left him?
   A. T. Ray made Lily kneel down on grits.
   B. T. Ray lost himself for a bit and confused Lily with Deborah.
   C. T. Ray hit Lily and told her she would never leave him again.
   D. T. Ray threatened Lily with a knife.

11. What brings T. Ray back to his senses?
   A. Rosaleen hits him with a broom.
   B. Lily hits him with a book.
   C. Lily yells at him, "Daddy!"
   D. August slams the door.

12. What declaration does Lily make to T. Ray?
   A. She tells him her mother is dead, and there is nothing either of them can do about that fact.
   B. She tells him she will never love him.
   C. She tells him she will not go back with him.
   D. She tells him he has lost.

13. Who comes to help Lily in her struggle against T. Ray?
   A. Zach comes, followed by August and Rosaleen.
   B. August and June come, followed by Rosaleen and Zach.
   C. June and Neil come, followed by August, Rosaleen, and the Daughters of Mary.
   D. August and Rosaleen come, followed by the other available Daughters of Mary.

14. What does August do to help diffuse the situation between T. Ray and Lily?
   A. She invites T. Ray to stay to dinner, to talk about things and to calmly straighten things out. She warmly welcomes him into her home and is clearly willing to share Lily with him.
   B. She starts talking to T. Ray about Deborah and the early, happier days of their marriage.
   C. She brings out the hat box with Deborah's things in it and offers it to T. Ray.
   D. She gives him a way out of the situation by saying he would be doing them a favor to let Lily stay.

15. Lily runs after T. Ray as he leaves, yelling for him to stop. What does she ask him, and what is his response?
   A. Lily asks him if she really did kill her mother. He tells her she did.
   B. Lily asks him if she can come visit him sometimes. He says, "Yes."
   C. Lily asks him what her favorite color is. He says, "Blue."
   D. Lily asks him if he loves her at all. He tells her he does not.

16. Who is Becca?
   A. Becca is a niece of the calendar sisters who sometimes comes by to visit with Lily.
   B. Becca is Clayton Forrest's daughter who sometimes comes by to visit with Lily.
   C. Becca is Zach's sister who sometimes comes by to visit with Lily.
   D. Becca is Neil's sister who sometimes comes by to visit with Lily.

17. What are Becca and Lily called at school? Why?
   A. They are called "the rainbow girls" because they associate with people of any color.
   B. They are called "Daughters of Mary" because they officially joined the group.
   C. They are called "the bee girls" because they work with August doing the bees.
   D. They are called "nigger lovers" because they associate with Zach at school.

18. What is the closing image of the novel?
   A. The queenless bee colony has found a new queen.
   B. Lily is looking into the sunrise.
   C. The women in Lily's life are standing strongly behind her.
   D. Our Lady of Chains smiles.

ANSWER KEY: STUDY QUESTIONS *The Secret Life of Bees*

	1	2	3	4	5	6	7	8	9	10	11
1	D	D	A	C	B	C	B	B	B	D	C
2	D	A	B	A	C	D	B	B	A	C	A
3	A	A	A	A	A	A	D	D	B	D	D
4	B	C	D	A	A	C	A	B	C	B	B
5	C	A	B	B	C	C	A		B	A	D
6	D	C	D	D	A	B	D		B		D
7	C	B	B	C	D		D		B		C
8	A	B	A	A					A		C
9	B	D	B	C					D		B
10	C	A	C	B							A
11	C		A	C							C
12	C		B								C
13	A		A								D
14	C										D
15	C										A
16	C										B
17	C										D
18	B										C
19	D										

VOCABULARY WORKSHEETS

VOCABULARY ASSIGNMENT 1 *The Secret Life of Bees*

Part I: Using Prior Knowledge and Contextual Clues

Below are the sentences in which the vocabulary words appear in the text. Read the sentence. Use any clues you can find in the sentence combined with your prior knowledge, and write what you think the underlined words mean on the lines provided.

1. I know it is presumptuous to compare my small life to hers, but I have reason to believe she wouldn't mind. . . .

   ____

2. I decided I would take four or five centuries to tell her about the special misery of living with T. Ray. He had an orneriness year-round, but especially in the summer when he worked his peach orchards daylight to dusk.

   ____

3. Still, the sight was a true spectacle. Suddenly, I couldn't stand not showing it off to somebody, even if the only person around was T. Ray.

   ____

4. My first and only memory of my mother was the day she died. I tried for a long time to conjure up an image of her before that, ...

   ____

5. Her hair was black and generous, with thick curls circling her face, a face I could never quite coax into view, despite the sharpening of everything else.

   ____

6. When she stepped in the room, her scent floated out to me, dark and spicy like the snuff she packed inside her cheek.

   ____

7. She'd thrown her husband out three years after they married, for carousing.

   ____

8. Once when he stepped on a roach in the kitchen, he told me my mother had spent hours luring roaches out of the house with bits of marshmallow and trails of graham-cracker crumbs, that she was a lunatic when it came to saving bugs.

   ____

9. Naturally the third man felt obliged to say something, so he looked at Rosaleen sashaying along unperturbed, holding her white-lady fan, ...

   ____

10. Naturally the third man felt obliged to say something, so he looked at Rosaleen sashaying along unperturbed, holding her white-lady fan, ...

    ____

The Secret Life of Bees Vocabulary Worksheet Assignment 1 Continued

Part II: Determining the Meaning -- Match the vocabulary words to their dictionary definitions.

____ 1.	PRESUMPTUOUS	A.	Create from nothing, as if by magic
____ 2.	ORNERINESS	B.	Something to be witnessed because of its impressive nature
____ 3.	SPECTACLE	C.	Excessively forward or confident
____ 4.	CONJURE	D.	Gently persuade
____ 5.	COAX	E.	Not disturbed; not bothered; unruffled
____ 6.	SNUFF	F.	Walking with a sway of the hips that intends to attract attention
____ 7.	CAROUSING	G.	Drunken merrymaking
____ 8.	LURING	H.	Tobacco in the form of powder, taken by sniffing it
____ 9.	SASHAYING	I.	Offering something tempting in order to persuade
____ 10.	UNPERTURBED	J.	Stubborn and irritable attitude

VOCABULARY ASSIGNMENT 2 *The Secret Life of Bees*

Part I: Using Prior Knowledge and Contextual Clues

Below are the sentences in which the vocabulary words appear in the text. Read the sentence. Use any clues you can find in the sentence combined with your prior knowledge, and write what you think the underlined words mean on the lines provided.

1. "I can't say what men riled up like that will do."

   ____

2. A brazen feeling had broken loose in me, a daring something that had been locked up in my chest.

   ____

3. Pious people have always gotten on my nerves.

   ____

4. "You can curse me, but don't blaspheme the Lord Jesus."

   ____

5. New beekeepers are told that the way to find the elusive queen is by first locating her circle of attendants.

   ____

6. We were to offer them the five-part plan of salvation, which they could accept or not.

   ____

The Secret Life of Bees Vocabulary Worksheet Assignment 2 Continued

Part II: Determining the Meaning -- Match the vocabulary words to their dictionary definitions.

____ 1.	RILED	A. Bold
____ 2.	BRAZEN	B. Provoked to anger
____ 3.	PIOUS	C. Deeply religious
____ 4.	BLASPHEME	D. Difficult to find, catch, or understand
____ 5.	ELUSIVE	E. Speak of something sacred in an irreverent manner
____ 6.	SALVATION	F. Preservation or deliverance from evil or difficulty

VOCABULARY ASSIGNMENT 3 *The Secret Life of Bees*

Part I: Using Prior Knowledge and Contextual Clues

Below are the sentences in which the vocabulary words appear in the text. Read the sentence. Use any clues you can find in the sentence combined with your prior knowledge, and write what you think the underlined words mean on the lines provided.

1. Twice she disappeared in the fogged billows, then gradually reemerged like a dream rising up from the bottom of the night.

 ____

2. June flounced out, her red skirt flashing around the door.

 ____

3. The growth turned thick, and sticker bushes snagged my legs, ...

 ____

4. I watched the currents meander, the lazy ripples that once in a while broke along the surface.

 ____

5. She played music for dying people, going to their homes and even to the hospital to serenade them into the next life.

 ____

6. This was a great revelation--not that I was white but that it seemed like June might not want me here because of my skin color.

 ____

7. Jesus had righteous indignation when he turned over the tables in the temple and drove out the thieving moneychangers.

 ____

8. He filled us in on an integration parade in St. Augustine that got attacked by a mob of white people, about white vigilante groups, fire hoses, and teargas.

 ____

9. "My mother was a good Catholic--she went to mass twice a week at St. Mary's in Richmond, but my father was an Orthodox Eclectic."

 ____

10. Anger agitates, while whistling melts a bee's temper.

 ____

11. August had been stung so many times she had immunity.

 ____

12. I watched her face flare with light, then recede into the dimness.

 ____

The Secret Life of Bees Vocabulary Worksheet Assignment 3 Continued

Part II: Determining the Meaning -- Match the vocabulary words to their dictionary definitions.

____ 1.	BILLOWS	A.	Moved casually and leisurely, with no direct route
____ 2.	FLOUNCED	B.	Those who punish lawbreakers themselves instead of relying upon official legal authority
____ 3.	SNAGGED	C.	Sing or perform a moving musical piece for a specific person
____ 4.	MEANDER	D.	Newly-discovered information, especially surprising information
____ 5.	SERENADE	E.	Moved with exaggerated motions expressive of displeasure or impatience
____ 6.	REVELATON	F.	Stirs up
____ 7.	INDIGNATION	G.	Rolling clusters of something such as smoke
____ 8.	VIGILANTE	H.	Caught by a sharp point
____ 9.	ECLECTIC	I.	Anger due to injustice or unreasonable action
____ 10.	AGITATES	J.	Made up of elements from several unlike sources
____ 11.	IMMUNITY	K.	Exemption or protection from danger
____ 12.	RECEDE	L.	Lessen or become distant

VOCABULARY ASSIGNMENT 4 *The Secret Life of Bees*

Part I: Using Prior Knowledge and Contextual Clues

Below are the sentences in which the vocabulary words appear in the text. Read the sentence. Use any clues you can find in the sentence combined with your prior knowledge, and write what you think the underlined words mean on the lines provided.

1. I thought about explaining to her my mother's ingenious method of ridding the house of roaches--cracker crumbs and marshmallow. . . .

   ____

2. How did bees ever become equated with sex? They do not live a riotous sex life themselves.

   ____

3. A hive suggests cloister more than bordello.

   ____

4. A hive suggests cloister more than bordello.

   ____

5. "How much further?" I said in a way that suggested the excursion could not be over too soon.

   ____

6. I remembered the pleasure of fainting that day during the Daughters of Mary meeting and thought now how much I would like to keel over right here in the truck.

   ____

7. She said that was because honey remnants attracted roaches.

   ____

The Secret Life of Bees Vocabulary Worksheet Assignment 4 Continued

Part II: Determining the Meaning -- Match the vocabulary words to their dictionary definitions.

____ 1.	INGENIOUS		A.	Place of religious seclusion and meditation
____ 2.	RIOTOUS		B.	House of prostitution
____ 3.	CLOISTER		C.	Loud, unrestrained behavior
____ 4.	BORDELLO		D.	Collapse or fall
____ 5.	EXCURSION		E.	Short trip
____ 6.	KEEL		F.	Small leftover amounts
____ 7.	REMNANTS		G.	Clever and original

VOCABULARY ASSIGNMENT 5 *The Secret Life of Bees*

Part I: Using Prior Knowledge and Contextual Clues

Below are the sentences in which the vocabulary words appear in the text. Read the sentence. Use any clues you can find in the sentence combined with your prior knowledge, and write what you think the underlined words mean on the lines provided.

1. She closed her eyes and soaked it in the way you imagine people at a fancy orchestra concert drinking up highbrow music.

   ____

2. Then the whole side of my face started to vibrate . . . I could see August's skin pulsating the tiniest bit.

   ____

3. I told her the way they created hexagons, they must be the ones who could do math in their heads, and she smiled and said, yes, nest builders had true math aptitude.

   ____

4. The only males were the drones who sat around waiting to mate with the queen.

   ____

5. . . . and it washed over me for the first time in my life just how much importance the world had ascribed to skin pigment, ...

   ____

6. I have always wanted to say to you that was DESPICABLE.

   ____

7. Y--YOKE AROUND MY NECK

   ____

The Secret Life of Bees Vocabulary Worksheet Assignment 5 Continued

Part II: Determining the Meaning -- Match the vocabulary words to their dictionary definitions.

____ 1.	HIGHBROW	A.	Device encircling the necks of a pair of oxen, mules, or other draft animals walking in a team; a restrictive or repressive force
____ 2.	PULSATING	B.	Horrible; deserving only contempt
____ 3.	APTITUDE	C.	Male bees that mate with the queen
____ 4.	DRONES	D.	Attributed to a particular cause, source, or origin
____ 5.	ASCRIBED	E.	Cultural and intellectual
____ 6.	DESPICABLE	F.	Natural talent or ability
____ 7.	YOKE	G.	Expanding and contracting in a certain pattern

VOCABULARY ASSIGNMENT 6 *The Secret Life of Bees*

Part I: Using Prior Knowledge and Contextual Clues

Below are the sentences in which the vocabulary words appear in the text. Read the sentence. Use any clues you can find in the sentence combined with your prior knowledge, and write what you think the underlined words mean on the lines provided.

1. The whole fabric of honey bee society depends on communication--on an innate ability to send and receive messages, to encode and decode information.

   ____

2. She pulled out a small bottle of olive oil and bee pollen from her free pocket and rubbed my skin--her patented remedy.

   ____

3. The sting shot pain all the way to my elbow, causing me to marvel at how much punishment a miniscule creature can inflict.

   ____

4. I was seeing myself as the fire department and June as the raging inferno.

   ____

5. We went to our knees, wrestling for it, the geyser weaving between us, her eyes staring at me, close and bright with beads of water on her eyelashes.

   ____

6. Some people might see it as shiftless behavior, but really, when we're lying down from the heat, we're giving our minds time to browse around for new ideas, ...

   ____

7. Sometimes things of magnitude settle over you with excruciating slowness.

   ____

8. May had turned back to her work. She seemed oblivious to me sitting there.

   ____

9. . . . I was suspended, waiting, caught in a terrible crevice between living my life and not living it.

   ____

The Secret Life of Bees Vocabulary Worksheet Assignment 6 Continued

Part II: Determining the Meaning -- Match the vocabulary words to their dictionary definitions.

____ 1.	INNATE	A.	Lazy
____ 2.	PATENTED	B.	Completely unaware
____ 3.	MINISCULE	C.	Extremely painful
____ 4.	INFERNO	D.	Registered as one's own unique idea, process, or product
____ 5.	GEYSER	E.	Possessed at birth; inborn
____ 6.	SHIFTLESS	F.	Tiny
____ 7.	EXCRUCIATING	G.	Narrow crack
____ 8.	OBLIVIOUS	H.	Place of a fiercely burning fire
____ 9.	CREVICE	I.	Spring that regularly, forcefully ejects a stream of hot water or steam up into the air

VOCABULARY ASSIGNMENT 7 *The Secret Life of Bees*

Part I: Using Prior Knowledge and Contextual Clues

Below are the sentences in which the vocabulary words appear in the text. Read the sentence. Use any clues you can find in the sentence combined with your prior knowledge, and write what you think the underlined words mean on the lines provided.

1. During spring and summer--the most strenuous periods of foraging--a worker bee, as a rule, does not live more than four or five weeks.

   ____

2. See? You aren't the only one who can concoct lies at the drop of a hat.

   ____

3. "Sometimes people have a hard time letting death sink in, they can't say good-bye. A vigil helps us do that."

   ____

4. I could not believe how quickly she crossed the grass with her loping strides, her long legs stretched out under her skirt.

   ____

5. She smiled at me in a way that made me feel I was about to get Part Two of the beekeeper's induction, Part One being the sting.

   ____

6. I turned to August, who was wiping her eyes from tears of hilarity.

   ____

The Secret Life of Bees Vocabulary Worksheet Assignment 7 Continued

Part II: Determining the Meaning -- Match the vocabulary words to their dictionary definitions.

____ 1.	FORAGING	A.	Extreme funniness
____ 2.	CONCOCT	B.	Characterized by long, easy strides
____ 3.	VIGIL	C.	Searching for food
____ 4.	LOPING	D.	Process of introducing someone to a group
____ 5.	INDUCTION	E.	Invent; make up
____ 6.	HILARITY	F.	An all-night event spent watching, praying, or guarding

VOCABULARY ASSIGNMENT 8 *The Secret Life of Bees*

Part I: Using Prior Knowledge and Contextual Clues

Below are the sentences in which the vocabulary words appear in the text. Read the sentence. Use any clues you can find in the sentence combined with your prior knowledge, and write what you think the underlined words mean on the lines provided.

1. . . . I'd been falling into lazy habits without the honey house to keep me industrious.

____

2. The smell of fresh-baked cake wafted all the way from the pink house to my cot, curled around my nostrils, and woke me up.

____

3. We had all these chores facing us, but some things you have to sit and mull over before you can go on.

____

4. He wouldn't have wasted time fainting, just gotten busy arranging the exorcism.

____

5. I glanced at poor, shackled Mary. I couldn't bear seeing her like that.

____

6. The cicadas were going crazy, filling the air with their strange brand of singing.

____

The Secret Life of Bees Vocabulary Worksheet Assignment 8 Continued

Part II: Determining the Meaning -- Match the vocabulary words to their dictionary definitions.

____ 1.	INDUSTRIOUS	A. Process of releasing evil spirits from a place or person
____ 2.	WAFTED	B. Large, winged insect; males make a high-pitched, droning noise
____ 3.	MULL	C. Chained
____ 4.	EXORCISM	D. Hard-working
____ 5.	SHACKLED	E. Moved or floated gently through the air
____ 6.	CICADAS	F. Consider; think deeply about

VOCABULARY ASSIGNMENT 9 *The Secret Life of Bees*

Part I: Using Prior Knowledge and Contextual Clues

Below are the sentences in which the vocabulary words appear in the text. Read the sentence. Use any clues you can find in the sentence combined with your prior knowledge, and write what you think the underlined words mean on the lines provided.

1. If the queen were smarter, she would probably be hopelessly neurotic.

____

2. As it is, she is shy and skittish, possibly because she never leaves the hive, but spends her days confined in darkness, a kind of eternal night, perpetually in labor . . . .

____

3. As it is, she is shy and skittish, possibly because she never leaves the hive, but spends her days confined in darkness, a kind of eternal night, perpetually in labor . . . .

____

4. Her true role is less that of a queen than mother of the hive, a title often accorded to her.

____

5. I must have been too muddled then to see it, because it all seemed new to me.

____

6. I was sniffling, wiping my cheeks, unable to stop my mouth from spewing out every horrible thing I could drum up about myself, ...

____

7. You think you want to know something, and then once you do, all you can think about is erasing it from your mind. From now on when people asked me what I wanted to be when I grew up, I planned to say, Amnesiac.

____

The Secret Life of Bees Vocabulary Worksheet Assignment 9 Continued

Part II: Determining the Meaning -- Match the vocabulary words to their dictionary definitions.

____ 1.	NEUROTIC	A. Continually; always; without end
____ 2.	SKITTISH	B. Overanxious or oversensitive about trivial occurrences
____ 3.	PERPETUALLY	C. Easily frightened
____ 4.	ACCORDED	D. Confused
____ 5.	MUDDLED	E. Forcing out in a stream
____ 6.	SPEWING	F. Given to
____ 7.	AMNESIAC	G. Someone who cannot remember

VOCABULARY ASSIGNMENT 10 *The Secret Life of Bees*

Part I: Using Prior Knowledge and Contextual Clues

Below are the sentences in which the vocabulary words appear in the text. Read the sentence. Use any clues you can find in the sentence combined with your prior knowledge, and write what you think the underlined words mean on the lines provided.

1. I hadn't moved since August left, only lay there staring at the flat surface of the wall, at the array of night bugs that wander out and crawl around for fun after they think you're asleep.

   ____

2. You want the one you're praying to at least to look capable.

   ____

3. --a statue of Mary with a wide-open door and, inside, all these people tucked away in the secret world of consolation.

   ____

4. I stood numb and plaster stiff in the corner of the kitchen.

   ____

5. Inside, I felt small and contemptible, abandoned.

   ____

6. I eliminated the one about multiplying loaves and fishes, as I never wanted to see food again.

   ____

The Secret Life of Bees Vocabulary Worksheet Assignment 10 Continued

Part II: Determining the Meaning -- Match the vocabulary words to their dictionary definitions.

____ 1.	ARRAY	A. Able; competent
____ 2.	CAPABLE	B. Without feeling
____ 3.	CONSOLATION	C. Got rid of
____ 4.	NUMB	D. Comfort; cheer in a time of grief, defeat, or trouble
____ 5.	CONTEMPTIBLE	E. Undeserving of respect
____ 6.	ELIMINATED	F. Large number or variety

VOCABULARY ASSIGNMENT 11 *The Secret Life of Bees*

Part I: Using Prior Knowledge and Contextual Clues

Below are the sentences in which the vocabulary words appear in the text. Read the sentence. Use any clues you can find in the sentence combined with your prior knowledge, and write what you think the underlined words mean on the lines provided.

1. A queenless colony is a pitiful and melancholy community; there may be a mournful wail or <u>lament</u> from within . . . .

   ____

2. A queenless colony is a pitiful and <u>melancholy</u> community; there may be a mournful wail or lament from within . . . .

   ____

3. If you see bees <u>loafing</u> and lamenting, you can bet their queen is dead.

   ____

4. I remember thinking that he probably loved me in his own smallish way. He had <u>forfeited</u> me over, hadn't he?

   ____

5. August says [this Mary] goes into the holes life has <u>gouged</u> out of us.

   ____

The Secret Life of Bees Vocabulary Worksheet Assignment 11 Continued

Part II: Determining the Meaning -- Match the vocabulary words to their dictionary definitions.

____ 1.	LAMENT	A.	Gave up something willingly
____ 2.	MELANCHOLY	B.	Expression of grief
____ 3.	LOAFING	C.	With a gentle sadness
____ 4.	FORFEITED	D.	Spending time in a lazy way
____ 5.	GOUGED	E.	Cut or scooped holes in something

VOCABULARY ANSWER KEY - *The Secret Life of Bees*

	1	2	3	4	5	6	7	8	9	10	11
1	C	B	G	G	E	E	C	D	B	F	B
2	J	A	E	C	G	D	E	E	C	A	C
3	B	C	H	A	F	F	F	F	A	D	D
4	A	E	A	B	C	H	B	A	F	B	A
5	D	D	C	E	D	I	D	C	D	E	E
6	H	F	D	D	B	A	A	B	E	C	
7	G		I	F	A	C			G		
8	I		B			B					
9	F		J			G					
10	E		F								
11			K								
12			L								

DAILY LESSONS

LESSON ONE

Objectives

1. To introduce students to subject matter discussed in the novel
2. To introduce students to a variety of media center resources or online research
3. To distribute books and other materials necessary for the unit

Activity 1
Meet in the library or media center.

Explain to students that the class will be reading Sue Monk Kidd's *The Secret Life of Bees,* and distribute the materials students will use in this unit. Explain in detail how students are to use these materials.

Books
Each school has its own rules and regulations regarding student use of school books. Advise students of the procedures that are normal for your school. Preview the book. Look at the covers, front matter, and index.

Study Guides
Students should read the study guide questions for each reading assignment prior to beginning the reading assignment to get a feeling for what events and ideas are important in the section they are about to read. After reading the section, students will (as a class or individually) answer the questions to review the important events and ideas from that section of the book. Students should keep the study guides as study materials for the unit test.

Vocabulary
Prior to each reading assignment, students will do vocabulary work related to the section of the book they are about to read. Following the completion of the reading of the book, there will be a vocabulary review of all the words used in the vocabulary assignments. Students should keep their vocabulary work as study materials for the unit test.

Reading Assignment Sheet
You need to fill in the reading assignment sheet to let students know by when their reading has to be completed. You can either write the assignment sheet up on a side blackboard or bulletin board and leave it there for students to see each day, or you can make copies for each student to have. In either case, you should advise students to become very familiar with the reading assignments so they know what is expected of them.

Extra Activities Center
The Unit Resource Materials portion of this LitPlan contains suggestions of topics for an extra library of related books and articles in your classroom as well as crossword and word search puzzles. Make an extra activities center in your room where you will keep these materials for students to use. (Bring the books and articles in from the library and keep several copies of the puzzles on hand.) Explain to students that these materials are available for students to use when they finish reading assignments or other class work early.

Non-fiction Assignment Sheet
Explain to students that they each are to read at least one non-fiction piece from the in-class library at some time during the unit. Students will fill out a non-fiction assignment sheet after completing the reading to help you (the teacher) evaluate their reading experiences and to help the students think about and evaluate their own reading experiences.

Activity 2

Explain to students that there are allusions to many different things in The *Secret Life of Bees,* and today they will explore some of those things so that when they come upon them in the text, they'll get the allusion.

Divide students into groups of three. Each group should receive an Allusion Bingo board. When told to begin, students will have about 20 minutes to research the terms on their cards by using library resources or the internet. As they define a particular term, they should write down notes of identification on the Allusion Bingo Terms page (or a separate sheet of plain paper if you prefer) and place a sticker on (or mark over) that square on the card.

Let students decide how to divide up the work. The first team to complete its card (find information about all of the terms or get 5 in a row if you choose to play Bingo) will receive a "free jar of honey" (whatever prize you decide to give).

After the teams have completed their tasks, bring everyone back together to discuss the terms on the cards.

NON-FICTION ASSIGNMENT SHEET
(To be completed after reading the required non-fiction article)

Name ________________________________ Date________________

Title of Non-fiction Read_______________________________________

Written By _______________________ Publication Date ___________

I. Factual Summary: Write a short summary of the piece you read.

II. Vocabulary

1. With which vocabulary words in the piece did you encounter some degree of difficulty?

2. How did you resolve your lack of understanding with these words?

III. Interpretation: What was the main point the author wanted you to get from reading his work?

IV. Criticism

1. With which points of the piece did you agree or find easy to accept? Why?

2. With which points of the piece did you disagree or find difficult to believe? Why?

V. Personal Response: What do you think about this piece? <u>OR</u> How does this piece influence your ideas?

B	I	N	G	O
Our Lady of the Chains	Gabriel and Mary	Honeycomb	*The Fugitive*	Jack Palance
The Beatles	Emily Dickenson	*$64,000 Question*	Bomb drills	Civil Rights Act
President Johnson	"Go Tell It on the Mountain"	FREE SPACE	Jim Crow	Sunbeam Bread
Shirley Temple	Martha White	Kruschev	Sophia Loren	Martin Luther King, Jr. arrested
"Stopping by Woods on a Snowy Evening"	"Oh, Susanna"	Madonna	Charm Bracelet	African-American Voter Registration

ALLUSION BINGO TERMS

The Secret Life of Bees

TERM	EXPLANATION OF TERM
Our Lady of Chains	
Gabriel and Mary	
Honeycomb	
The Fugitive	
Jack Palance	
The Beatles	
Emily Dickenson	
The $64,000 Question	
Bomb Drills	
Civil Rights Act	
President Johnson	
"Go Tell It On The Mountain"	

TERM	EXPLANATION OF TERM
Jim Crow	
Sunbeam Bread	
Shirley Temple	
Martha White	
Kruschev	
Sophia Loren	
Martin Luther King, Jr. Is Arrested	
"Stopping By The Woods On A Snowy Evening"	
"Oh, Susanna"	
Madonna (not the singer)	
Charm Bracelet	
African-American Voter Registration	

LESSON TWO

Objectives

1. To preview the study questions for Chapter 1
2. To preview the vocabulary for Chapter 1
3. To read Chapter 1
4. To evaluate students' oral reading
5. To give students practice reading orally

Activity 1
Explain to students that just prior to each reading assignment, they will have some pre-reading work to do, including previewing the study questions and completing a vocabulary worksheet. Explain that these activities will help prepare them to get more out of their reading.

Tell students to look at their study guide questions for the first reading assignment, Chapter 1. Read the questions orally with students, then explain that these questions point out some of the key facts or ideas in the story that they should look for when reading.

Activity 2
Tell students to look at the vocabulary worksheet for the first reading assignment, Chapter 1. Explain to students that completing this worksheet will help them better understand the words when they come upon them as they read.

In the first part of the worksheet, students should try to guess the meaning of the words using prior knowledge and any contextual clues. Do the first part of the worksheet orally with your students.

In the second part of the worksheet, students should match the words with their correct definitions. You may do this orally together as a class activity or allow students time to complete this part independently and then check the answers as a class. Students should use contextual clues and the process of elimination to narrow the choices for the words, then, if they still aren't sure of the correct definition(s), students should look up the word(s) in a dictionary.

Explain to students that there is one worksheet for each reading assignment, and these worksheets will always be completed prior to reading the assignments.

These worksheets can be checked or graded each time the class discusses the answers to the study questions for the same assignment, or, if your students don't need the in-class reinforcement, you could just post the correct answers on the board each day and students can check their own papers when they come in to class.

Activity 3
Begin reading Chapter 1 aloud in class. You could read it to your students, you could play a audio recording of it, or you could have your students take turns reading. If you have a lower level class, reading to or playing a recording for your students might be a good way to start the unit to help get them interested. Then, have students read orally on a different assignment later in the unit.

If you have not yet completed an oral reading evaluation for your students yet this term, this is a good opportunity to do so. A form is enclosed for your convenience.

If you do not finish reading Chapter 1 during the class time, students should complete reading the assignment prior to the next class meeting.

ORAL READING EVALUATION- *The Secret Life of Bees*

Name ____________________________ Class___ Date ___________

SKILL	EXCELLENT	GOOD	AVERAGE	FAIR	POOR
Fluency	5	4	3	2	1
Clarity	5	4	3	2	1
Audibility	5	4	3	2	1
Pronunciation	5	4	3	2	1
________	5	4	3	2	1
________	5	4	3	2	1

Total _____ Grade

Comments:

LESSON THREE

Objectives

1. To bring two events out of the book and into the classroom
2. To briefly discuss and/or review the terms "diction," "denotation," and "connotation" as they apply to characterizatoin
3. To review the main events and ideas from Chapter 1
4. To preview the study questions and do the vocabulary work for Chapters 2 and 3
5. To read Chapters 2 and 3
6. To evaluate students' oral reading

Activity 1

This activity requires you to bring both grits and a charm bracelet to class.

Do a mini-demonstration of the "Martha Whites" punishment. Some students may not be familiar with grits, which has tradionally been a southern food staple. "Martha Whites" used to be a leading brand of grits, but any brand of grits will work for this demonstration.

Empty a bag (or box) of grits into a large, flat container. Grits should layer approximately an inch deep. Ask for a few volunteers to come press the knuckles of their fists into the layer of grits (for about 1-2 minutes each) using as much pressure as possible. Discuss the results. Discuss how Lily must have felt kneeling on the grits, and discuss what this punishment tells us about T. Ray.

Students may benefit from seeing an actual charm bracelet, which Lily desperately wants. Not many people actually "collect" charms for charm bracelets anymore, but it was quite a fad in the past. If you can find one, show it to your students and let them pass it around and look at it. Explain that girls would get a charm bracelet and perhaps one or two charms for a birthday or other special occasion, then they would buy (or get for presents) other charms to go on it, over a number of years. The charms would generally be of things that interested the girl. For example, a girl who took dance lessons might get a little ballerina charm. One who played the piano might get a little piano charm, and so on. Some popular vacation places used to offer charms as souvenirs. For example, one might get a Statue of Liberty charm while on vacation in New York City. The girl would continue adding as many charms as possible, and when the bracelet was "full" some girls added another one and wore them together.

Ask students what the equivallent "fad" is today. What item do most teenagers desperately want now? Ask students how they think people will view that item several decades from now.

Activity 2

If students are not familiar with the literary term "DICTION," explain that basically it is an author's word choice. (You might relate DICTion with DICTionary or contraDICTion to help explain.)

Write the following sentence on the board: *A man walked down the street*. Give students a minute to write down as much as they can about the man, his mood, his attitude, what he is thinking, etc. Discuss students' responses, making sure that they provide evidence for their conclusions. Likely, the students will have few details to add because the sentence provides little opportunity for inference.

Now, write the word "WALK" in the center of the board. Ask a student to quickly look up the word in a dictionary. Record a concise verb form of the definition next to the word "WALK." Explain a word's definition is known as the "DENOTATION" of that word. Ask students to brainstorm as many synonyms for the word "WALK" as they can.

Next, ask for volunteers to DEMONSTRATE one of the synonyms used. For example, if "STRUT" is offered as a response, ask a volunteer to STRUT across the classroom. Substitue the word "struts" for "walked" in the sentence on the board. Ask students what could be inferred about the man by the fact that he is "strutting" down the street instead of merely "walking." Does the word "strutting" characterize the man in a particular way? If so, how? Substitute some of the other synonyms given and discuss each.

Explain that the impression that a word gives is the "CONNOTATION" of that word. Brainstorm and discuss additonal examples. A few follow to get you started:

-- talk, chatter, blab, lecture
-- smell, odor, scent, aroma
-- eat, gulp, devour, nibble
-- look, flirt, stare, glare
-- hit, tap, pound, smack
-- cry, weep, sob, wail
-- smile, smirk, grin, sneer
-- bandit, thug, robber, hustler

Near the end of Chapter 1, the author says ". . . he looked at Rosaleen *sashaying* along unperturbed . . . ." Why was "sashaying" selected instead of "walking"? What connotations does the word "sashaying" have? How does the word characterize Rosealeen? Is there any other word that would have had the same effect?

Tell students to keep an eye out for these kinds of words throughout their reading in this book. Tell them that an author's word choice is very important and that they should be conscious of using words with the correct connotations when they speak and write.

This would also be a good time to show students a thesarus and how to use it if they don't already know.

EXTRA PRACTICE:
An optional extra practice worksheet follows this lesson. It is here for your convenience in case some or all of your students need extra practice with the concept of diction and characterization.

<u>Activity 3</u>
Give students a few minutes to formulate answers for the study guide questions for Chapter 1, then discuss the answers to the questions in detail. Write the answers on the board or overhead transparency so students can have the correct answers for study purposes. WHEN YOU FINISH ANSWERING THE QUESTIONS FOR CHAPTER 1, PREVIEW THE QUESTIONS FOR CHAPTERS 2-3.

NOTE: It is a good practice in public speaking and leadership skills for individual students to take charge of leading the discussions of the study questions. Perhaps a different student could go to the front of the class and lead the discussion each day that the study questions are discussed in this unit. Of course, you should guide the discussion when appropriate and try to fill in any gaps students may leave.

The study questions could really be handled in a number of different ways, including in small groups with group reports following. Occasionally you may want to use the multiple choice questions as quizzes to check students' reading comprehension.

As a short review now and then, students could pair up for the first (or last, if you have time left at the end of a class period) few minutes of class to quiz each other from the study questions.

Mix up the methods of reviewing the materials and checking comprehension throughout the unit so students don't get bored just answering the questions the same way each day. Variety in methods will also help address the different learning styles of your students.

From now on in this unit, the directions will simply say, "Discuss the answers to the study questions in detail as previously directed." You will choose the method of preparation and discussion each day based on what best suits you and your class.

Activity 4
Do the vocabulary worksheet for Chapters 2-3 together orally in class.

Activity 5
Read Chapters 2-3 orally in class for the remainder of the class period. If you have not yet done or completed oral reading evaluations for your students this term, this is a good opportunity to do so.

If you do not finish reading Chapters 2-3 in class, students should complete the assignment prior to the next class meeting.

DICTION AND CHARACTERIZATION

Directions: Substitute words with distinct connotations for the underlined words.
Example: The man walked down the street. The man *strolled* down the street.

1. A man came from the seats behind me. (A)

2. A man came from the seats behind me. (A)

3. A man came from the seats behind me. (A)

4. He smiled at me as he walked by. (B)

5. He smiled at me as he walked by. (B)

6. I looked at him going away. (C)

7. I looked at him going away. (C)

8. A man stopped him before he left. (D)

9. A man stopped him before he left. (D)

10. A man stopped him before he left. (D)

Rewrite the story in 4 sentences (A, B, C, and D) using the words you substituted for the underlined words.

LESSON FOUR

Objectives

1. To further discuss characterization
2. To examine the characters we have met so far in the book
3. To review the main events and ideas from Chapters 2-3
4. To preview the study questions and vocabulary for Chapters 4-5
5. To read Chapters 4-5

Activity 1

Remind the class that yesterday you discussed DICTION, DENOTATION, CONNOTATION, and CHARACTERIZATION. Briefly review the material covered in the last class period asking students for definitions and examples of the terms covered.

Tell students that the connotative words the author chooses are one element that help us to know and understand a character, but there are other things that are important, too: the character's physical description, the character's personality, how the character interacts with others, and the things that are said by and about the character also build the character in readers' minds.

Take a few minutes to look at some of the characters we have met so far in the book. Divide your students into groups of three to five students. Assign each group one of the characters in chapters 1-3, and give each group a CHARACTER MAP worksheet to complete. Let students work on it for about fifteen minutes before coming back together as a class to discuss the results.

Students should:

1. Write the character's name in the center circle

2. Look in the text for words giving a physical description of the character and note them in the top-left box along with the page number where the descriptive words were found

3. Identify the character's relationship with others in the book and note those relationships in the top-right box

4. In the bottom-left box, list key words describing the character's personality and cite the pages/passages on which they based their choice of the key words

5. Cite at least one quote from the book that is key to helping the reader understand the character

At this point in time, students could do character maps for Lily, Rosaleen, or T. Ray. After students have had time to work on their maps and dig around in the text, come back together as a class, discuss what students have found. Make notes on your board, in a character map layout, so students can copy important information for studying purposes.

FOLLOW UP:

As students read more of the book, they should complete character maps for May, June, and August as well as Deborah, Zach, Neil, the Daughters of Mary, and Clayton Forrest. A small amount of class time is set aside for working on these, but your students may need more or less direction and time than allowed in this unit. You'll need to adjust accordingly.

Activity 2
Discuss the answers to the study questions for Chapters 2-3 as previously directed.

While students have their study guides out, preview the study questions for Chapters 4-5.

Activity 3
Students need to do the vocabulary worksheet for Chapters 4-5 prior to reading the assignment. If you are continuing with the oral reading (and oral reading evaluations), it would be best to do the vocabulary together orally in class. If students will be reading Chapters 4-5 silently, the vocabulary work could be done independently. Direct your students accordingly.

Activity 4
Students should read Chapters 4-5. If you are doing the oral reading evaluations and have not yet completed them, try to do so now. If you have completed (or aren't doing) the oral reading evaluations, students may read Chapters 4-5 silently.

This reading assignment should be completed prior to the next class meeting.

CHARACTER MAP
The Secret Life of Bees

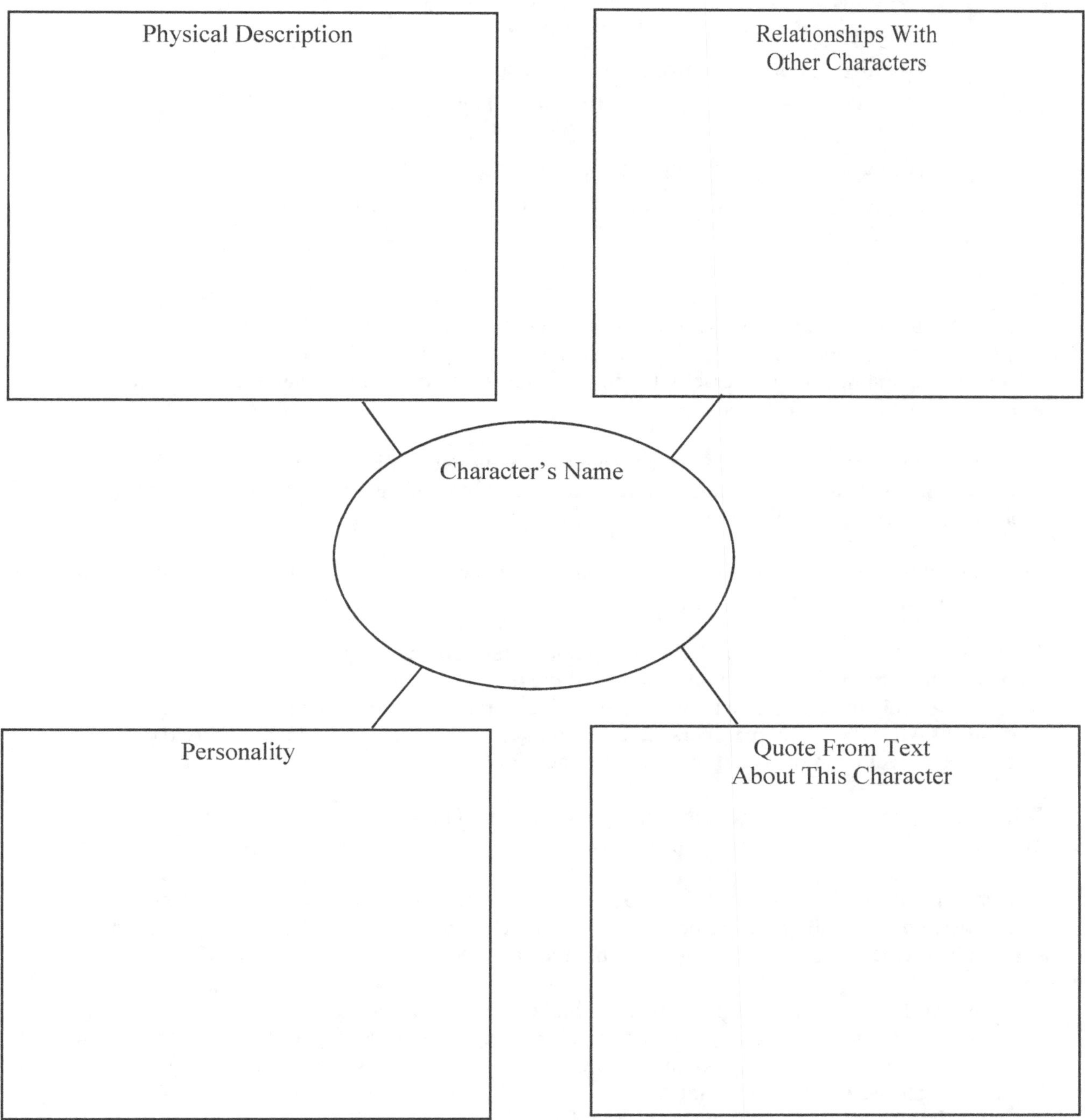

1. Write the character's name in the center circle
2. Look in the text for words giving a physical description of the character and note them in the top-left box along with the page number where the descriptive words were found
3. Identify the character's relationship with others in the book and note those relationships in the top-right box
4. In the bottom-left box, list key words describing the character's personality and cite the pages/passages on which you based your choice of the key words
5. Cite at least one quote from the book that is key to helping the reader understand the character

LESSON FIVE

Objectives

1. To define types of figurative language and literary devices
2. To identify figurative language in the text
3. To utilize graphic organizers for comprehension
4. To explore how the author uses figurative language to help create the characters and the story
5. To review the main events and ideas of Chapters 4-5
6. To preview the study questions and vocabulary for Chapters 6-7
7. To read Chapters 6-7

Activity 1

Explain to students that in the last few lessons we have discussed the author's use of individual words (denotation, connotation) as well as the characters' physical descriptions, their personalities, and how they interact with others in the story to build the characters in readers' minds.

Another tool writers use (not only for character development but also for plot and theme development) is *figurative language*. There are many kinds of figurative language. Today we will look at onomatopoeia, simile, metaphor, personification, and imagery.

Distribute the Literary Devices worksheet. Discuss each of the types of figurative language and their definitions.

Divide students into groups, one for each type of literary device, about 5 students to a group. Each student in the group should take one chapter of the book (1-5), look for examples of that literary device in that chapter, and note their examples (including the page numbers) on the back of the worksheet. After the group members have found several examples, they should share their findings and decide on the best two examples they found.

When the groups are done, have each group report its two best examples to the rest of the class so all students can fill in the worksheet.

Ask students if they were surprised at the number of examples of these devices they found in the novel. Ask why they think the author used so many. How is the novel enhanced or hurt by the use of such language? Does it seem plausable that the characters would speak this way?

OPTIONAL HOMEWORK: Develop an original example of figurative language for each of the following: metaphor, simile, personification, onomatopoeia, hyperbole. For students who require more challenging assignments, ask them to develop TWO examples of figurative language for each of the terms. The first one should be something Shakespeare might have used, while the second might be one used by Larry the Cable Guy.

Activity 2

Discuss the answers to the study questions for Chapters 4-5 as previously directed.

Preview the questions for Chapters 6-7 while students have their study guides out.

Activity 3

If you have completed the oral reading evaluations, students may do the vocabulary work for

Chapters 6-7 independently and then read Chapters 6-7 silently for the remainder of the class period.

If you have not completed the oral reading evaluations or if you simply choose to have students read aloud (or to use an audio recording), do the vocabulary worksheet for Chapters 6-7 together as a class followed by the reading.

If students do not complete the reading assignment in class, they should do so prior to the next class period.

LITERARY DEVICES - *The Secret Life of Bees*

1. Review each of the literary devices.
2. Find a passage in *The Secret Life of Bees* that demonstrates Kidd's use of each device (be sure to include the page number for each passage).
3. Explain how the passage demonstrates the use of each literary device.

Literary Device	**Definition**	**Example from Novel**	**Explanation**
Example: Onomatopoeia	Use of a word whose sound imitates or suggests its meaning	"the *swish* of the clothes," "wire *clinking* together," "the *buzzing* of the bees" (p. 6)	When they move, clothes make a sound much like the sound of the word "swish." When wire hits together, it produces a sound much like the word "clink." Bees make a sound like the sound of the word "buzz."
onomatopoeia	Use of a word whose sound imitates or suggests its meaning		
simile	Explicit comparison of two essentially unlike things, usually stated using "like" or "as"		
metaphor	A word or phrase that ordinarily designates one thing is used to designate another, thus making an implicit comparison		
personification	Giving human qualities to inanimate objects		
Hyperbole	An exaggeration or extravagant statement used as a figure of speech		

FIGURATIVE LANGUAGE in *The Secret Life of Bees*
(Penguin Edition)

ONOMATOPOEIA

. . . making that propeller sound, a high-pitched *zzzzzz* that hummed along my skin. (1)

. . . and the electric percolator bubbled into the tiny glass nozzle on top of it. *Bloop, bloop.* I loved the way it sounded, the way it smelled. (102)

June made a *pfffff* sound with her lips while August shook her head . . . . (154)

You come over here and you gonna get wet, she said, and *splat*! We were hit full in the chest with ice-cold water. (168)

I could barely hear them over the bamming of my heart. (194)

Outside the window a crow flew past, filling the bathroom with a frantic *caw-caw*, and Rosaleen stopped, waiting for it to die down. (263)

SIMILE

I watched their wings shining like bits of chrome in the dark . . . .1)

Every one of those bees could have descended on me like a flock of angels . . . . (2)

Rosaleen looked straight ahead and acted as if the men were insignificant houseflies buzzing at our screen door. (35)

. . . I took the pillows from underneath the bedspread and placed them around me like I was making an inner tube that might keep me afloat. I could understand her leaving him. But leaving *me*? This would sink me forever.(40)

. . . said Rosaleen, laying into each [profane] word like it was sweet potatoes on her tongue. (49)

A barge of mist floated along the water, and dragonflies, iridescent blue ones, darted back and forth like they were stitching up the air. (57)

Twice she disappeared in the fogged billows, then gradually reemerged like a dream rising up from the bottom of the night. (67)

. . . suddenly May started to sob. Of course everybody jumped up like she was an unpinned grenade and tried to quiet her, but it was too late. (89)

I'd seen the plague of locusts at the movies, the sky filled with hordes of insects looking like kamikaze planes. (151)

. . . I'd tried to imagine people crouched outside, bobbing along peacefully like a rubber duck in a child's bathtub, . . . (165)

When we got up, June said, "Lord, I feel woozy, like somebody has pulled the plugs in my feet and drained me out." (169)

We walked along the river with the words streaming behind us like ribbons in the night. (191)

Something about this caused my own eyes to sting like sand had flown into them. (249)

I hated feeling like a concrete block in the middle of the night. (258)

My heart beat wildly. I felt like I'd unzipped my skin and momentarily stepped out of it, leaving a crazy person in charge. (259)

The room turned like a carousel, with my stomach gliding up and down. (259)

[Deborah's hair] had grown out of her head and now perched there like a thought she had left behind on the brush. (273)

METAPHOR

The way those bees flew…split my heart down its seam. (1)

I could tell by the way her eyes rolled under her lids she was watching the silver screen where dreams come and go. (58)

I could make out about fourteen beehives tucked under the trees in the distance, the tops of them postage stamps of white shine. (79)

What I mean is that the bees weren't *really* singing the words from Luke, but still, if you have the right kind of ears, you can listen to a hive and hear the Christmas story somewhere inside yourself. (144)

We had our ears pressed to a giant music box. (148)

I peeled the gloves from my sweaty hands and felt a wave of jitteriness, the old saw-edged guilt, the necklace of lies I could not stop wearing, the fear of being cast out of the pink house. (171)

Looking at [August's] eyes, I could see a fire inside them. It was a hearth fire you could depend on, you could draw up to and get warm by if you were cold, or cook something on that would feed the emptiness in you. I felt like we were all adrift in the world, and all we had was the wet fire in August's eyes, (181)

It was plain Rosaleen had a fire in her, too. Not a hearth fire, like August, but fire that burns the house down, if necessary, to clean up the mess inside it. (182)

Rosaleen reminded me of the statue of Our Lady in the parlor, and I thought, *If August is the red heart on Mary's chest, Rosaleen is the fist.* (182)

[May's hands] floated, her palms little ragged cups bobbing on the surface, . . . (193)

Twice I walked into a spider's web, feeling the fine, transparent threads across my face, and I liked them there. A veil spun from the night. (229)

All these mothers. I have more mothers than any eight girls off the street. They are the moons shining over me. (302)

PERSONIFICATION

His boots whispered uncle all the way down the hall. (12)

I wanted to lie down in the orchard and let it hold me. (22)

In the autumn South Carolina changed her color to ruby red and wild shades of orange. (300)

HYPERBOLE

I sat on a Coke crate and watched pickups zoom by till I was nearly poisoned with exhaust fumes and boredom. (15)

LESSON SIX

Objectives

1. To define the term "allusion" and its various types
2. To demonstrate how an author's use of allusion contributes to characterization and theme development
3. To examine the quality of literature and define criteria for evaluating literature and writing
4. To review the main events and ideas in Chapters 6-7
5. To preview the study questions and vocabulary for Chapter 8
6. To read Chapter 8

Activity 1

Write the word "allusion" on the board. Give students an opportunity to offer definitions for this term. Explain that in **literature, an allusion is a reference to a famous person, place, thing, piece of literature, art, music, etc., that the reader is expected to recognize**.

Ask students to provide examples of allusions they have encountered in previous literature study. What allusions can we find in the everyday world? (For example, mythological allusions abound--such as Ajax cleanser and King Triton from Disney's *The Little Mermaid*). Allow the class to brainstorm as many allusions from as many different sources as they can.

TRANSITION:
In *The Secret Life of Bees*, the author uses many allusions. How many can you recall without looking back at the text? On the board, write the examples students give. (Students might remember doing the allusions worksheet at the beginning of the unit. Those examples are good, too!)

Have students break into seven groups, one for each chapter the class has read so far. Students should work together to find examples of allusions in their assigned chapters and write down the references and the page numbers.

After students have had about 10 minutes to find the allusions, bring the class back together for a whole-class discussion. The discussion may include inquiries such as: Why might the author have chosen these particular allusions for this particular novel? How does the use of the allusions affect a reader's understanding of a theme, character, or episode in the novel? Consider all the ways that allusions are used in *The Secret Life of Bees*. What impact might alternate choices have made on the reader's overall impression of the themes or characters? What does the breadth and variety of the allusions used tell us about the author? What do the allusions add to the story? Do they make it better? What criteria should we use to determine what constitutes good literature? Does it matter? What should be the ultimate determination of whether a book is used in a classroom? Do you think *The Secret Life of Bees* is a good choice?

Tell students to continue to notice allusions used in the text as they continue to read the rest of the book.

Activity 2

Discuss the study question answers for Chapters 6-7 as previously directed.

Preview the study questions for Chapter 8 while students have their study guides out.

Activity 3
If you have completed the oral reading evaluations, students may do the vocabulary work for Chapter 8 independently and then read Chapter 8 silently for the remainder of the class period.

If you have not completed the oral reading evaluations or if you simply choose to have students read aloud (or to use an audio recording), do the vocabulary worksheet for Chapter 8 together as a class followed by the reading.

If students do not complete the reading assignment in class, they should do so prior to the next class period.

List of Allusions - *The Secret Life of Bees*

<u>Religion</u>
Gabriel and Mary (2)
Wailing Wall- Jerusalem (97)
"Amazing Grace" (110)
"Go Tell It On the Mountain" (111)
Moses…Egypt (151)
Hail Mary's (151)

<u>Literature</u>
Emily Dickenson (16)
Shakespeare (57)
Walden Pond (57)
"Alice in Wonderland" (171)
"Stopping by Woods on a Snowy Evening" (237)
William Blake (274)

<u>Newspaper topics (1964)</u>
Malcolm X (66)
Beatles (66)
Jackson, MS- segregation (66)
Beatles (66)
Wimbledon tennis (66)
Saigon (66)

<u>People</u>
Sophia Loren (9)
Thomas Edison (41)
Walter Cronkite (88)
Zachary Taylor (116)
John F. Kennedy (163)
Will Chamberlain (183)
Shirley Temple (246)
Johnson and Humphrey (283)

<u>Culture/Entertainment/Music</u>
Uncle Wiggly (5)
$64,000 Question
Supremes (219)
Ozzie and Harriet (94)
Elvis (116)
"Blueberry Hill (116)
"Viva Las Vegas (116)
Ed Sullivan (185)
American Bandstand (175)
Sam Cooke (176)
"Another Saturday Night" (176)
"Oh, Susanna" (73)
Fats Domino (117)
The Fugitive (123)
Nat King Cole (155)
"Unforgettable " (285)
Jack Palance (154)

<u>History</u>
Mr. Kruchchev (20)
President and Lady Bird Johnson (20)
Martin Luther King, Jr.- arrest (21)
Eleanor Roosevelt (57)
General Sherman (61)
Blue Laws (60)
Fort Sumter (65)
Santa Maria/Columbus (70)
Four girls killed in Birmingham (80)
Niagra Falls- barrels (165)
Kamikaze planes (151)
St. Augustine integration parade (88)
Reference to victims like Emmett Till (135)

LESSON SEVEN

Objectives

1. To discuss the epigraphs and their relationship to the plot
2. To review the main events and ideas in Chapter 8
3. To preview the study questions and vocabulary for Chapter 9
4. To read Chapter 9

Activity 1
Explain to students that epigraphs are the mottos or quotations used at the beginning of each chapter. Write the epigraph for the first chapter on the board:

The queen, for her part, is the unifying force of the community; if she is removed from the hive, the workers very quickly sense her absence. After a few hours, or even less, they show unmistakable signs of queenlessness. --Man and Insects

Ask students to recount the events that happened in Chapter 1, then discuss how the epigraph relates to those events.

Distribute the Epigraph Worksheet. Decide whether you want students to complete the worksheet independently, in groups, or as a whole class, and instruct them accordingly.

If you do not do the worksheet together as a whole class, give students about 15 minutes to work on the assignment.

Explain to students that they should continue completing the worksheet as they read each remaining chapter in the book. (You may want to add the epigraph discussion when you do the study questions for each remaining chapter.)

Activity 2
Discuss the answers to the study questions for Chapter 8 as previously directed.

Preview the study questions for Chapter 9 while students have their study guides out.

Activity 3
If you have completed the oral reading evaluations, students may do the vocabulary work for Chapter 9 independently and then read Chapter 9 silently for the remainder of the class period.

If you have not completed the oral reading evaluations or if you simply choose to have students read aloud (or to use an audio recording), do the vocabulary worksheet for Chapter 9 together as a class followed by the reading.

If students do not complete the reading assignment in class, they should do so prior to the next class period.

EPIGRAPHS – *The Secret Life Of Bees*

Chapter	Epigraph	Brief Summary of the Chapter	Parallel Between Epigraph and the Plot
1	The queen, for her part, is the unifying force of the community; if she is removed from the hive, the workers very quickly sense her absence. After a few hours, or even less, they show unmistakable signs of queenlessness. *–Man and Insects*		
2	On leaving the old nest, the swarm normally flies only a few metres and settles. Scout bees look for a suitable place to start the new colony. Eventually, one location wins favor and the whole swarm takes to the air. *–Bees of the World*		
3	New beekeepers are told that the way to find the elusive queen is by first locating her circle of attendants. *–The Queen Must Die: And Other Affairs of Bees and Men*		
4	Honeybees are social insects and live in colonies. Each colony is a family unit, comprising a single, egg-laying female or queen and her many sterile daughters called workers. The workers co-operate in the food-gathering, nest-building, and rearing the off-spring. Males are reared only at the times of year when their presence is required. *–Bees of the World*		
5	Let's imagine for a moment that we are tiny enough to follow a bee into a hive. Usually the first thing we would have to get used to is the darkness. . . *–Exploring the World of Social Insects*		
6	The queen must produce some substance that attracts the workers and that can be obtained from her only by direct contact. This substance evidently stimulates the normal working behavior in the hive. This chemical messenger has been called "queen substance." Experiments have shown that the bees obtain it directly from the body of the queen. *–Man and Insects*		
7	How did bees ever become equated with sex? They do not live a riotous sex life themselves. A hive suggests cloister more than bordello. *–The Queen Must Die: And Other Affairs of Bees and Men*		

The Secret Life of Bees Epigraphs Continued

8	Honeybees depend not only on physical contact with the colony, but also require its social companionship and support. Isolate a honeybee from her sisters and she will soon die. –*The Queen Must Die: And Other Affairs of Bees and Men*		
9	The whole fabric of honey bee society depends on communication—on an innate ability to send and receive messages, to encode and decode information. –*The Honey Bee*		
10	A bee's life is but short. During spring and summer—the most strenuous periods of foraging—a worker bee, as a rule, does not live more than four or five weeks . . . Threatened by all kinds of dangers during their foraging flights, many workers die before they have reached even that age. –*The Dancing Bees*		
11	It takes honeybee workers ten million foraging trips to gather enough nectar to make one pound of honey. –*Bees of the World*		
12	If the queen were smarter, she would probably be hopelessly neurotic. As is, she is shy and skittish, possibly because she never leaves the hive, but spends her days confined in darkness, a kind of eternal night, perpetually in labor. . . . Her true role is less that of a queen than mother of the hive, a title often accorded to her. And yet, this is something of a mockery because of her lack of maternal instincts or the ability to care for her young. –*The Queen Must Die: And Other Affairs of Bees and Men*		
13	A worker [bee] is just over a centimeter long and weighs only about sixty milligrams; nevertheless, she can fly with a load heavier than herself. –*The Honey Bee*		
14	A queenless colony is a pitiful and melancholy community; there may be a mournful wail or lament from within. . . . Without intervention, the colony will die. But introduce a new queen and the most extravagant change takes place. –*The Queen Must Die: And Other Affairs of Bees and Men*		

LESSON EIGHT

Objectives

1. To explore the historical context of the novel
2. To compare and analyze accounts of the same incident with regard to purpose and effect
3. To review the main events and ideas of Chapter 9
4. To preview the study questions and vocabulary for Chapter 10
5. To read Chapter 10

Activity 1

Ask students what they know about the historical context of the novel, the Civil Rights movement in the early 1960's. Ask students how they know about these things: from what sources have they acquired their information? What are some sources of information about this time period? Build a discussion based on students' responses.

TRANSITION:

As we have discussed, we receive information about events from many different sources: newspapers, songs, books, television programs, and much more. It is important to realize how those who write or create these things influence our perception of the events. To explore this idea a little more, we're going to look at two different accounts of an event mentioned in the novel.

One piece of paper May stuck into her wall said, "Birmingham, Sept. 15, four little angels dead." Discuss how those words make the readers feel.

Distribute the newspaper account of the incident at the church. Either read it to your students, or have students read it to each other. Discuss the article in detail. Compare and contrast its effect with the effect of the wailing wall note May wrote.

Distribute the *Ballad of Birmingham*. Read it with your students. How is its effect different from the newspaper article and from May's note?

How might the purpose of a news article differ from the purpose of a literary piece? How might the purpose of non-fiction differ from the purpose of fiction?

Point out that we need to be aware that the words we read and hear manipulate how we view events. Likewise, as writers, we can also use words to create our own desired effects.

Activity 2

Discuss the study questions for Chapter 9 as previously directed. While students have their study guides out, preview the questions for Chapter 10.

Activity 3

Students have three assignments to complete prior to the next class period:

They should complete the pre-reading vocabulary worksheet for Chapter 10.

They should read Chapter 10.

They should bring in an article from this week's newspaper--any article from any section of the paper--to use as a basis for their own works of historical fiction.

Six Dead After Church Bombing

Blast Kills Four Children; Riots Follow Two Youths Slain; State Reinforces Birmingham Police

United Press International
September 16, 1963

Birmingham, Sept. 15 -- A bomb hurled from a passing car blasted a crowded Negro church today, killing four girls in their Sunday school classes and triggering outbreaks of violence that left two more persons dead in the streets.

Two Negro youths were killed in outbreaks of shooting seven hours after the 16th Street Baptist Church was bombed, and a third was wounded.

As darkness closed over the city hours later, shots crackled sporadically in the Negro sections. Stones smashed into cars driven by whites.

Five Fires Reported
Police reported at least five fires in Negro business establishments tonight. A official said some are being set, including one at a mop factory touched off by gasoline thrown on the building. The fires were brought under control and there were no injuries.

Meanwhile, NAACP Executive Secretary Roy Wilkins wired President Kennedy that unless the Federal Government offers more than "picayune and piecemeal aid against this type of bestiality" Negroes will "employ such methods as our desperation may dictate in defense of the lives of our people."

Reinforced police units patrolled the city and 500 battle-dressed National Guardsmen stood by at an armory.

City police shot a 16-year-old Negro to death when he refused to heed their commands to halt after they caught him stoning cars. A 13-year-old Negro boy was shot and killed as he rode his bicycle in a suburban area north of the city.

Police Battle Crowd
Downtown streets were deserted after dark and police urged white and Negro parents to keep their children off the streets.

Thousands of hysterical Negroes poured into the area around the church this morning and police fought for two hours, firing rifles into the air to control them.

When the crowd broke up, scattered shootings and stonings erupted through the city during the afternoon and tonight.

The Negro youth killed by police was Johnny Robinson, 16. They said he fled down an alley when they caught him stoning cars. They shot him when he refused to halt.

The 13-year-old boy killed outside the city was Virgil Ware. He was shot at about the same time as Robinson.

Shortly after the bombing police broke up a rally of white students protesting the desegregation of three Birmingham schools last week. A motorcade of militant adult segregationists apparently en route to the student rally was disbanded.

Police patrols, augmented by 300 State troopers sent into the city by Gov. George C. Wallace, quickly broke up all gatherings of white and Negroes. Wallace sent the troopers and ordered 500 National Guardsmen to stand by at Birmingham armories.

King arrived in the city tonight and went into a conference with Rev. Fred Shuttlesworth, a leader in the civil rights fight in Birmingham.

The City Council held an emergency meeting to discuss safety measures for the city, but rejected proposals for a curfew.

Dozens of persons were injured when the bomb went off in the church, which held 400 Negroes at the time, including 80 children. It was Young Day at the church.

A few hours later, police picked up two white men, questioned them about the bombing and released them.

The Rev. Martin Luther King Jr. wired President Kennedy from Atlanta that he was going to Birmingham to plead with Negroes to "remain non-violent."

But he said that unless "immediate Federal steps are taken" there will be "in Birmingham and Alabama the worst racial holocaust this Nation has ever seen."

Dozens of survivors, their faces dripping blood from the glass that flew out of the church's stained glass windows, staggered around the building in a cloud of white dust raised by the explosion. The blast crushed two nearby cars like toys and blew out windows blocks away.

Negroes stoned cars in other sections of Birmingham and police exchanged shots with a Negro firing wild shotgun blasts two blocks from the church. It took officers two hours to disperse the screaming, surging crowd of 2,000 Negroes who ran to the church at the sound of the blast.

At least 20 persons were hurt badly enough by the blast to be treated at hospitals. Many more, cut and bruised by flying debris, were treated privately.

(The Associated Press reported that among the injured in subsequent shooting were a white man injured by a Negro. Another white man was wounded by a Negro who attempted to rob him, according to police.)

Mayor Albert Boutwell, tears streaming down his cheeks, announced the city had asked for help.

"It is a tragic event," Boutwell said. "It is just sickening that a few individuals could commit such a horrible atrocity. The occurrence of such a thing has so gravely concerned the public..." His voice broke and he could not go on.

Boutwell and Police Chief Jamie Moore requested the State assistance in a telegram to Wallace.

"While the situation appears to be well under control of federal law enforcement officers at this time, the possibility of further trouble exists," Boutwell and Moore said in their telegram.

President Kennedy, yachting off Newport, R.I., was notified by radio-telephone and Attorney General Robert F. Kennedy ordered his chief civil rights troubleshooter, Burke Marshall, to Birmingham. At least 25 FBI agents, including bomb experts from Washington, were being rushed in.

City Police Inspector W.J. Haley said as many as 15 sticks of dynamite must have been used.

"We have talked to witnesses who say they saw a car drive by and then speed away just before the bomb hit," he said.

In Montgomery, Wallace said he had a similar report and said the descriptions of the car's occupants did not make clear their race. But he served notice "on those responsible that every law enforcement agency of this State will be used to apprehend them."

The bombing was the 21st in Birmingham in eight years, and the first to kill. None of the bombings have been solved.

As police struggled to hold back the crowd, the blasted church's pastor, the Rev. John H. Cross, grabbed a megaphone and walked back and forth, telling the crowd: "The police are doing everything they can. Please go home."

"The Lord is our shepherd," he sobbed. "We shall not want."

The only stained glass window in the church that remained in its frame showed Christ leading a group of little children. The face of Christ was blown out.

After the police dispersed the hysterical crowds, workmen with pickaxes went into the wrecked basement of the church. Parts of brightly painted children's furniture were strewn about in one Sunday School room, and blood stained the floors. Chunks of concrete the size of footballs littered the basement.

The bomb apparently went off in an unoccupied basement room and blew down the wall, sending stone and debris flying like shrapnel into a room where children were assembling for closing prayers following Sunday School. Bibles and song books lay shredded and scattered through the church.

In the main sanctuary upstairs, which holds about 500 persons, the pulpit and Bible were covered with pieces of stained glass.

One of the dead girls was decapitated. The coroner's office identified the dead as Denise McNair, 11; Carol Robertson, 14; Cynthia Wesley, 14, and Addie Mae Collins, 10.

As the crowd came outside watched the victims being carried out, one youth broke away and tried to touch one of the blanket-covered forms.

"This is my sister," he cried. "My God, she's dead." Police took the hysterical boy away.

Mamie Grier, superintendent of the Sunday School, said when the bomb went off "people began screaming, almost stampeding" to get outside. The wounded walked around in a daze, she said.

One of the injured taken to a hospital was a white man. Many others cut by flying glass and other debris were not treated at hospitals.

Fourth in Four Weeks

It was the fourth bombing in four weeks in Birmingham, and the third since the current school desegregation crisis came to a boil Sept. 4.

Desegregation of schools in Birmingham, Mobile, and Tuskegee was finally brought about last Wednesday when President Kennedy federalized the National Guard. Some of the Guardsmen in Birmingham are still under Federal orders. Wallace said the ones he alerted today were units of the Guard "not now federalized."

The City of Birmingham has offered a $52,000 reward for the arrest of the bombers, and Wallace today offered another $5,000.

Dr. King Berates Wallace

But Dr. King wired Wallace that "the blood of four little children ... is on your hands. Your irresponsible and misguided actions have created in Birmingham and Alabama the atmosphere that has induced continued violence and now murder."

Ballad of Birmingham
By Dudley Randall
(On the bombing of a church in Birmingham, Alabama, 1963)

"Mother dear, may I go downtown
Instead of out to play,
And march the streets of Birmingham
In a Freedom March today?"

"No, baby, no, you may not go,
For the dogs are fierce and wild,
And clubs and hoses, guns and jails
Aren't good for a little child."

"But, mother, I won't be alone.
Other children will go with me,
And march the streets of Birmingham
To make our country free."

"No, baby, no, you may not go,
For I fear those guns will fire.
But you may go to church instead
And sing in the children's choir."

She has combed and brushed her night-dark hair,
And bathed rose petal sweet,
And drawn white gloves on her small brown hands,
And white shoes on her feet.

The mother smiled to know her child
Was in the sacred place,
But that smile was the last smile
To come upon her face.

For when she heard the explosion,
Her eyes grew wet and wild.
She raced through the streets of Birmingham
Calling for her child.

She clawed through bits of glass and brick,
Then lifted out a shoe.
"O, here's the shoe my baby wore,
But, baby, where are you?"

LESSON NINE

Objectives

1. To evaluate students' understanding of the literary elements studied so far in this unit
2. To evaluate students' understanding of and ability to apply purpose in writing
3. To put into practice literary elements studied so far in this unit: figures of speech, connotations, allusions

Activity

Tell students to retrieve the newspaper articles they were to bring to class. Ask a few students to tell what their articles are about.

Explain to students that today they will create short works of historical fiction from the articles they have chosen. This is a creative writing assignment, but it also has to do with description and persuasion. Students should choose their words carefully to elicit the desired emotional response from their readers.

Distribute Writing Assignment #1 and discuss the directions in detail. Give students the remainder of this class time to work on this assignment. Tell students when their final drafts will be due.

Students who finish early may do the vocabulary worksheet for Chapter 11.

WRITING ASSIGNMENT #1 *The Secret Life of Bees*

PROMPT

Throughout *The Secret Life of Bees*, Sue Monk Kidd weaves historical events into her fictional storyline. Other writers, such as Dudley Randall, have also depicted social events in a literary framework ("Ballad of Birmingham"). Refer to the article that you selected from a newspaper or magazine. Your assignment is to use the facts of the article in a work of historical fiction, choosing your words carefully (using figurative language, connotation, allusions and other devices we have studied) to elicit the desired response from your readers.

PRE-WRITING

How might you represent the events of that article through historical fiction? What do you want to convey to your readers? What response do you want from your readers regarding the issues in your article? Will you write in prose or poetry? What point of view will you use in your piece? How do you want your readers to feel about the principal characters or events? Think a few minutes about these key questions and jot down your thoughts.

Your work of historical fiction must include examples of at least two different types of figurative language and two allusions. Think about what images or allusions might connect well with your work and jot them down.

Do you need to make up some additional characters? Maybe you need to embellish some facts? Consider the techniques you might use to strengthen the emotional power of the fictionalized piece you create. Make notes of your thoughts on these issues.

DRAFTING

Using your article, your notes, and your thoughts, write a rough draft of your work of historical fiction. There are many different ways of approaching this assignment, so no step-by-step directions are available, but put pen to paper and begin *somewhere*; you can (and should) always go back to revise, strengthen, and polish your work.

PROOFREADING

After you have revised and edited your work to the best of your ability, have someone whose opinions you trust proofread and evaluate your work. That person should let you know the good points as well as things that could be improved. Consider your critic's opinions and revise as you feel necessary, making a good, final copy to submit.

WRITING EVALUATION FORM - *The Secret Life of Bees*

Name ______________________________ Date ____________

Grade ____________

Circle One For Each Item:

Grammar:	correct errors noted on paper			
Spelling:	correct errors noted on paper			
Punctuation:	correct errors noted on paper			
Legibility:	excellent	good	fair	poor
_____________	excellent	good	fair	poor
_____________	excellent	good	fair	poor

Strengths:

Weaknesses:

Comments/Suggestions:

LESSON TEN

Objectives

1. To review the main events and ideas of Chapter 10
2. To preview the study questions and vocabulary for Chapter 11
3. To read Chapter 11

Activity 1

Discuss the study questions for Chapter 10 as previously directed. Preview the study questions for Chapter 11 while students have their study guides out.

Activity 2

Do the vocabulary worksheet for Chapter 11 orally together in class.

Activity 3

Give students the remainder of the class period to read Chapter 11. They may read silently, in pairs, in small groups, or as a class--whichever you choose.

LESSON ELEVEN

Objectives

1. To widen the breadth and depth of students' knowledge base
2. To preview the study questions and vocabulary for Chapter 12
3. To read Chapter 12
4. To explore topics related to the novel in more depth
5. To practice research skills

Activity

Take students to the library or media center. Give each student a different topic from the Related Topics list in the Unit Resource Materials section of this LitPlan. Some of these topics are duplicated from the Allusion Bingo activity in Lesson One; research on these topics at this time should be more in-depth.

Give each student 3 Non-fiction Assignment Sheets.

Students should read about their topics from at least three different sources, completing a Non-fiction Assignment Sheet for each.

Students should use the remainder of this class period to complete their research.

If students finish early, they should preview the study questions and do the vocabulary work for Chapter 12. Students should also read Chapter 12. This assignment should be completed prior to the next class meeting.

LESSON TWELVE

Objectives

1. To prepare students for making oral presentations
2. To review the main events and ideas from Chapters 11 & 12
3. To practice writing to inform
4. To preview the study questions and vocabulary for Chapter 13
5. To read Chapter 13

Activity 1

Discuss the study questions for chapters 11 & 12 as previously directed. Preview the questions for Chapter 13 while students have their study guides out.

Take the time to review the correct answers for the vocabulary worksheets for these chapters as well if you do not have a self-checking system for vocabulary already in place for students.

Activity 2

Students have researched and completed Non-fiction Assignment Sheets related to their research topics. In this class period, students will create a written report from their reading. In the next class, students will give brief oral reports about their topics. Doing this written work first will help prepare them for the oral presentations.

Distribute Writing Assignment #2, discuss the directions in detail, and give students ample time to complete the assignment.

WRITING ASSIGNMENT #2 *The Secret Life of Bees*

PROMPT
Through the initial activity of Allusion Bingo and through your research you have become more familiar with at least one topic related to *The Secret Life of Bees*. You personally cannot travel back in time, but you can send a message to Lily. Write a letter to her telling her about your assigned topic from your perspective today.

PRE-WRITING
You have already done most of the preparation for this assignment through your research. Review the Non-fiction Assignment Sheets you completed. On a separate page, write down any other notes you can think of about your topic--things you know from general knowledge or have heard.

How might you see this person, thing, or event differently from how Lily might have seen it? What do you know now from history that Lily could not have known? Take these things into consideration when you are writing to Lily.

DRAFTING
Your letter should have all the usual friendly letter parts (date, greeting, body, closing, and signature) and be in a friendly letter format:

Date

Greeting,

Paragraph 1--Write as many paragraphs as you need.

Paragraph 2--Write as many paragraphs as you need.

Closing,

Signature

Remember Lily is stuck in the early 1960's. Be careful not to use any allusions she would not know about (unless you explain them).

Write your first draft, then revise and polish it until you are satisfied with it.

PROOFREADING
After you have written the best letter you can, have someone whose opinions you trust read and evaluate your letter, letting you know the good points and things that could use improvement. Consider your critic's comments and make the necessary changes. Make a final draft to submit for grading.

LESSON THIRTEEN

Objectives

1. To practice public speaking
2. To expose all students to a wide variety of background information
3. To preview the study questions and vocabulary for Chapter 14
4. To read Chapter 14

Activity 1

Call on individual students to give their oral presentations about their topics. The presentations should be brief but thorough. Place a time limit on the presentations based on your total class time and/or the ability of your students.

Allow for a brief question and answer period at the end of the presentations. You can make this as elaborate or as simple as you choose, taking more than one class period if necessary. Some teachers find the related topics of little importance while others think the knowledge base it helps build to be very important. Use your time according to your own curriculum guidelines or personal preferences.

Activity 2

Students should preview the study questions and vocabulary for Chapter 14 and read Chapter 14 prior to the next class meeting. If time remains in class, students may begin this assignment.

LESSON FOURTEEN

Objectives

1. To review the main events and ideas of chapters 13 & 14
2. To examine characterization in the novel
3. To examine the relationship between point of view and characterization
4. To analyze connections between plot and characterization
5. To use additional sources of literature to draw conclusions about *The Secret Life of Bees*
6. To prepare students for Writing Assignment #3

Activity 1

Discuss the answers to the study questions for Chapters 13 & 14 as previously directed.

Don't forget to make sure students have the correct answers for the vocabulary worksheets for these sections, too.

Activity 2

You will need a copy of *The Three Little Pigs* (any version with third-person narration will do) and a copy of *The True Story of the Three Little Pigs* by Joh Scieszka and Lane Smith. Both are available for sale at www.tpet.com and www.amazon.com and may be available at the library. See bulletin board #15 in the Unit Resource Materials section of this LitPlan for an additional idea.

The point of this activity is to illustrate the importance of point of view.

Read *The Three Little Pigs* aloud. Have students join in on the parts they know so well. Afterwards, discuss the characters. Make a list of adjectives to describe each character in the story.

Next, read *The True Story of the Three Little Pigs*. Using a different color marker, list adjectives for the characters in that story. How do the two lists compare? What reasons can the students offer for the differences?

Activity 3

Review the major types of point of view:

1st person
2nd person
3rd person omniscient
3rd person limited

Generate examples for each type from readings you have conducted throughtout the year--or throughout your students' education. In which instances were the narrator and the point-of-view particularly important to the total effect of the literature?

Discuss from what point of view *The Secret Life of Bees* is told--and how that affects our perception of the events of the story (and thus the themes). What are the advantages and disadvantages of using this point of view for this story?

LESSON FIFTEEN

Objectives

1. To experiment with the effect of point of view on characterization and plot in *The Secret Life of Bees*
2. To review the literary tools discussed in this unit
3. To evaluate students' ability to use literary devices in their own writing

Activity 1

Take a few minutes to review the literary tools/techniques discussed in this unit.

Remind students that these are not the only tools in the writer's toolbox--just the ones we have paid close attention to in this unit.

Diction: denotation and connotation
Characterization through diction, description, action, interaction, and reaction
Figurative Language: onomatopoeia, simile, metaphor, personification, imagery
Allusions
Epigraphs
Point of View

When you discuss Point of View, transition into the writing assignment by discussing how Lily's point of view influences our opinions of T. Ray.

Was T. Ray such a horrible person and a terrible father? Discuss. Have students brainstorm specific scenes involving T. Ray and analyze his actions in each. On the board, make a list of the scenes discussed.

Activity 2

Distribute Writing Assignment #3 and discuss the directions in detail. Give students ample time to complete this assignment and tell them when it will be collected for grading.

WRITING ASSIGNMENT #3 *The Secret Life of Bees*

PROMP

We have discussed how an author uses point of view to influence readers' opinions of characters, events, and themes. Your assignment is to practice using this writing tool (as well as the other devices we have studied) by rewriting a scene from *The Secret Life of Bees* from T. Ray's point of view. You are to rewrite the scene when T. Ray comes to get Lily from the calendar sisters' home. In addition to rewriting the scene from T. Ray's point of view, you should also change it so T. Ray is as persuasive as possible trying to get Lily to come with him. You may end the scene any way you wish--with Lily going with him, or not.

PRE-WRITING

Think about the scene from T. Ray's point of view. What could cause him to act like this? What actually does he say or do that is so terrible, if anything? What emotions are revealed when T. Ray is granted a voice in this scene? Jot down some adjectives or phrases that could describe his feelings or emotions.

As the author, you are free to choose words and use literary devices. Jot down things you think T. Ray might say in this scene, ideas for descriptions, allusions, similies, metaphors, etc. you think might be useful as you rewrite the scene. Write down any reasons or ideas you have that T. Ray might use to persuade Lily to come with him.

Go back and re-read the scene in the novel paying particular attention to how the author begins the scene, develops it, and ends it. Jot down notes about how you might apply a similar process in your scene.

DRAFTING

Using your notes, begin writing. Make a rough draft then go back and revise it as many times as necessary to make the action and dialogue true to the characters and to make your word choices as effective as possible.

PROOFREADING

After you have made your scene as good as you can make it, have someone whose opinions you trust read and evaluate it, telling you the good points and things that could use improvement. Decide what revisions need to be made, make them, and write a final copy to submit.

LESSONS SIXTEEN AND SEVENTEEN

Objectives

1. To examine the themes of the novel more closely
2. To practice critical reading skills
3. To practice teamwork skills

Activity

One of the things that makes *The Secret Life of Bees* a good book is that it has many strands of themes running through it, weaving in and out. Use this class time to pull out those themes and examine them more closely.

One way to do this would be to divide your class into six groups, one for each of the following themes, issues, or ideas:

Religion
Mothers
Race Issues
Coping
Freedom
Choosing What Matters

Have students within the groups split up the book into sections. Each student should take one section, skim it to find references to the group's topic, and jot down page numbers & notes about the references. Worksheets for each group are on the following pages. After individual students have finished finding references, all group members should get together to discuss their findings and complete their worksheets.

Allow time either in this class meeting or the next one for the groups to give mini-reports and to allow class time for discussion of these important topics from *The Secret Life of Bees*.

GROUP WORKSHEET FOR THE THEME OF
RELIGION
in *The Secret Life of Bees*

List of Group Members (with assigned book chapters to skim for references):

1 ________________________________ Chapters ____________

2 ________________________________ Chapters ____________

3 ________________________________ Chapters ____________

4 ________________________________ Chapters ____________

5 ________________________________ Chapters ____________

6 ________________________________ Chapters ____________

7 ________________________________ Chapters ____________

ASSIGNMENT

Your group's assignment is to examine the topic of RELIGION throughout *The Secret Life of Bees*.

One group member should read this entire worksheet aloud with the group and lead the group through the work.

After reading through this worksheet, you will each skim through assigned chapters of the book to find references to this topic, jotting down the page number and a few notes about each reference you find.

After you all have completed your skimming and research, you will gather back together to discuss the things you have found and to complete the remainder of this worksheet.

You will then give a short presentation to the class and conduct a short discussion of this aspect of the novel with the class.

PROMPT

The American Heritage dictionary gives several definitions of the word "religion." Two that you should consider when doing this assignment follow:

1. The spiritual or emotional attitude of one who recognizes the existence of a superhuman power or powers.
2. Any objective attended to or pursued with zeal or conscientious devotion: *A collector might make a religion of his hobby.*

According to the first definition, you should look for all references to Mary, Jesus, church, and religion in the traditional church sense of the word. This would include activities of the Daughters of Mary, references to Gabriel, religious ceremonies or traditions, etc.

The second definition, however, gives us a broader sense of the word. Think about the characters of the book. Do any of them pursue any objective with zeal or conscientious devotion? Consider each of these characters and write down what, if anything, each pursues:

Lily

August

Neil

Zach

Now discuss this: Of those who pursue something, for which ones (if any) could the pursuit truly be considered a kind of a religion? Write down which things (if any) could be considered like a religion.

So, in addition to looking for references to religion in the traditional sense, also look for references to these religion-like activites.

RESEARCH

Now do your individual research. Each of you should skim through your chapters of the book to find references to RELIGION (as defined above) in the text. Write down the page number of each reference and a few notes to identify the reference.

GROUP DISCUSSION

When you finish finding references in your chapters, get together and discuss what you have found. Tell each other what you found and evaluate your findings. Which references are most relevant and seem most important in the overall picture of the book? Make a special note of these.

Based on the references you found in the text, discuss and answer the following questions:

1. Why/how is Lily's name symbolically important? With what are lilies associated?

FYI

Below are some other tidbits you can share with your classmates regarding the names of some characters in the book. You get to present them to the class because they mostly fit under the topic of religion.

<u>May</u>: Short version of the name Mary. In Catholicism, May is Mary's month, a month for special devotion to the Virgin Mary. The month of May was named for the Roman earth goddess, Maia.

<u>Raymond</u> (T. Ray): From the German meaning "protecting hands." St. Raymond of Nonnatus (who lived in the early 1200's) is the patron saint of expectant mothers and midwives, primarily because his own mother died giving birth to him.

<u>Rose</u> (Rosaleen): The rose is often used as a symbol for the Virgin Mary. "Rosa mystica" is another term for the Virgin Mary.

<u>Deborah</u>: Of Hebrew origin. Means "bee."

2. What, actually, is the point of all this stuff about the Virgin Mary in the book, in a religious sense?

3. In a sentence or two for each, define what "religion" means to or does for each of the following:
   Lily
   August
   Rosaleen
   Daughters of Mary

4. Discuss the incident where Rosaleen steals the fan from the church. Why is this event important, and what does it tell us about Rosaleen?

5. A lot of time in the book is spent on devotions, rituals, ceremonies, routines, and outward manifestations of "religion." However, in one of the most important passages of the book, August tells Lily that Mary is really on the *inside*. Using specific examples, explain what the outward manifistations of religion did for the characters involved.

6. Choose five references to religion from the text, ones you have not used in answering any of the above questions--and ones you think are the most important, and explain the importance of each.

   Reference 1 (page ___):

   Explanation:

   Reference 2 (page ___):

   Explanation:

   Reference 3 (page ___):

   Explanation:

Reference 4 (page ___):

Explanation:

Reference 5 (page ___):

Explanation:

7. For devotion to an activity, a hobby for example, to be considered a kind of a "religion," one's dedication to it has to be extraordinarily extreme. While August is certainly devoted to beekeeping and it is intertwined with religion in the book, one would be hard-pressed to truly classify it as a "religion." Discuss, however, how beekeeping *is* intertwined with religion in the book and give possible explanations as to why the author chose to do this.

8. Discuss and give a summary of the theme of RELIGION in the book *The Secret Life of Bees*.

ORAL PRESENTATION

You will be asked to give an oral presentation and lead a class discussion about the theme of religion in the book. Use this worksheet as a guide for your presentation.

At the end of your presentation, pose the following questions to your class:

1. Lily and Rosaleen do a whole lot of lying in the book, and they both break the law by stealing. Are these presented as bad things? Are bad things sometimes justifiable, and, if so, does that make them morally right--or simply commonly excusable?
2. In their devotions to Mary, the Daughters did a lot of praying. In the sketchy details given, it seems like they prayed the rosary or some form of it. Does anyone know what the rosary is or anything about it?

[FYI here is a short definition of the rosary you can share if no one knows anything about it:

The **Rosary** is a traditional Roman Catholic and Anglican devotion. The term denotes both a set of prayer beads used in the devotion and the devotional prayer itself. The Rosary is divided into five "decades." Each "decade" consists of one "Our Father" prayer followed by ten "Hail Mary" prayers and one "Glory Be" prayer, each designated by a series of large and small beads on a circular string. Each decade represents a mystery or event in the life of Jesus. There are four sets of "Mysteries of the Rosary" *(Joyful, Luminous, Sorrowful, and Glorious),* each with five decades, making a total of twenty mysteries (events). As one recites the prayers for each decade, one meditates on the "mystery" or event in the life of Jesus designated for that decade.

3. Had anyone heard of Black Madonnas before reading this book? [If so, ask how they heard about it.] Here is a little information you can share with the class:

Black Madonnas are statues or paintings of the Virgin Mary depicted with black or very dark skin tones. Most are dated to the 11th to 15th centuries and are from Catholic areas of Europe. They aren't a recent invention due to the Civil Rights movement in America; they have roots that go way back in history. If you're interested in seeing pictures or knowing more, just do an Internet search. There is a lot of information available.

4. Who has ever been to a funeral vigil? [Ask what went on at the vigils students have attended.] Here is some additional information you can share with your classmates about vigils.

Sitting with the deceased, keeping vigil, has been happening just about forever. Whether it was to pray for the deceased, to pay respects, to support the grieving family, or something as practical as keeping the body from being stolen, people have been keeping vigil for a very, very long time. It can take place at home or in a funeral parlor, and could be any amount of time from the time the person dies until burial takes place. Most modern vigils only last a short while, but a good old-fashioned wake could take place for days! The time spent could be very somber or quite a party, depending on the traditions of the family.

5. Ask if anyone has anything to add to the discussion of RELIGION in *The Secret Life of Bees* before you close the discussion, and field questions that may be asked.

GROUP WORKSHEET FOR THE THEME OF
MOTHERS/MOTHERHOOD
in *The Secret Life of Bees*

List of Group Members (with assigned book chapters to skim for references):

1 ________________________________ Chapters ____________

2 ________________________________ Chapters ____________

3 ________________________________ Chapters ____________

4 ________________________________ Chapters ____________

5 ________________________________ Chapters ____________

6 ________________________________ Chapters ____________

7 ________________________________ Chapters ____________

ASSIGNMENT

Your group's assignment is to examine the topic of MOTHERS throughout *The Secret Life of Bees*.

One group member should read this entire worksheet aloud with the group and lead the group through the work.

After reading through this worksheet, you will each skim through assigned chapters of the book to find references to this topic, jotting down the page number and a few notes about each reference you find.

After you all have completed your skimming and research, you will gather back together to discuss the things you have found and to complete the remainder of this worksheet.

You will then give a short presentation to the class and conduct a short discussion of this aspect of the novel with the class.

PROMPT

The Secret Life of Bees covers motherhood from the lowly queen bee to the Virgin Mary and everything in between. Mother figures abound. Think for minute about these questions and discuss them:

1. How many "mother" issues and relationships can you find in the book?

2. Which one is most *central* to the book?

RESEARCH

Now do your individual research. Each of you should skim through your chapters of the book to find references to MOTHERS in the text. Write down the page number of each reference and a few notes to identify the reference.

GROUP DISCUSSION

When you finish finding references in your chapters, get together and discuss what you have found. Tell each other what you found and evaluate your findings. Which references are most relevant and seem most important in the overall picture of the book? Make a special note of these.

Based on the references you found in the text, discuss and answer the following questions:

1. What do all the references to the Virgin Mary/Our Lady of Chains have to do with the theme of mother/motherhood in the novel?

2. Consider the following relationships with regard to the theme of mother/motherhood. What is the "bottom line" with regard to the theme of mother/motherhood for each?

   a. Lily and Deborah

   b. Lily and Rosaleen

   c. Lily and August

   d. Deborah and August

   e. August/June and May

   f. August and her grandmother

   g. Mary and the Daughters of Mary

   h. Lily and Mary

   i. August and Mary

   j. the queen bee and her colony

3. Choose five references to mother/motherhood from the text, ones you think are the most important, and explain the importance of each.

   Reference 1 (page ___):

   Explanation:

   Reference 2 (page ___):

   Explanation:

   Reference 3 (page ___):

   Explanation:

   Reference 4 (page ___):

   Explanation:

   Reference 5 (page ___):

   Explanation:

7. Discuss how beekeeping is intertwined with motherhood in the book and give possible explanations as to why the author chose to do this.

8. Discuss and give a summary of the theme of MOTHERS/MOTHERHOOD in the book *The Secret Life of Bees*.

ORAL PRESENTATION

You will be asked to give an oral presentation and lead a class discussion about the theme of motherhood in the book. Use this worksheet as a guide for your presentation.

At the end of your presentation, pose the following questions to your class:

1. Why is it so important to Lily to find out whether or not her mother really left her?
2. Lily needs to know if her mother really loved her. What difference do you think one answer or the other (whether she did or didn't) would make in Lily's life?
3. Does Lily *need* a mother?
4. What characteristics make a good mother?
5. Ask if anyone has anything to add to the discussion of MOTHERS/MOTHERHOOD in *The Secret Life of Bees* before you close the discussion, and field questions that may be asked.

GROUP WORKSHEET FOR THE THEME OF
CIVIL RIGHTS/RACE ISSUES
in *The Secret Life of Bees*

List of Group Members (with assigned book chapters to skim for references):

1 ______________________________ Chapters ____________

2 ______________________________ Chapters ____________

3 ______________________________ Chapters ____________

4 ______________________________ Chapters ____________

5 ______________________________ Chapters ____________

6 ______________________________ Chapters ____________

7 ______________________________ Chapters ____________

ASSIGNMENT

Your group's assignment is to examine the topic of RACE ISSUES throughout *The Secret Life of Bees.*

One group member should read this entire worksheet aloud with the group and lead the group through the work.

After reading through this worksheet, you will each skim through assigned chapters of the book to find references to this topic, jotting down the page number and a few notes about each reference you find.

After you all have completed your skimming and research, you will gather back together to discuss the things you have found and to complete the remainder of this worksheet.

You will then give a short presentation to the class and conduct a short discussion of this aspect of the novel with the class.

PROMPT

One important element of *The Secret Life of Bees* is its historical context and social commentary regarding civil rights and race issues.

Before doing your research, consider and discuss the following questions:

1. What incidents relating to your topic can you recall from the book?

2. What role do each of the following characters play in developing the theme(s) about race and civil rights in the book?

   Lily

   Rosaleen

   Zach

   August

   the Black Madonna

   Mr. Gaston

   June

   Mr. Hazelwurst

   Neil

   Clayton Forrest

   Becca

RESEARCH

Now do your individual research. Each of you should skim through your chapters of the book to find references to CIVIL RIGHTS/RACE ISSUES in the text. Keep in mind that references include incidents. You will have to "read between the lines" to find some references. Write down the page number of each reference and a few notes to identify the reference.

GROUP DISCUSSION

When you finish finding references in your chapters, get together and discuss what you have found. Tell each other what you found and evaluate your findings. Which references are most relevant and seem most important in the overall picture of the book? Make a special note of these.

Based on the references you found in the text, discuss and answer the following questions:

1. What does Our Lady of Chains have to do with the theme of civil rights and race in the novel?
2. What points about race relations does the author make using Lily's relationships with the following people?

   a. Rosaleen

   b. Zach

   c. August

   d. June

3. How is the setting of the book important to the theme of civil rights and race issues?

4. Compare and contrast Zach and Rosaleen with regard to their actions concerning race issues.

5. The author weaves historical events relating to civil rights and race issues into the fabric of the story. Give some examples of this and explain the value of using this technique.

6. What does the author suggest by the way the book was ended with regard to this theme?

7. Choose five references to civil rights and race issues from the text, ones you think are the most important, and explain the importance of each.

   Reference 1 (page ___):

   Explanation:

   Reference 2 (page ___):

   Explanation:

   Reference 3 (page ___):

   Explanation:

   Reference 4 (page ___):

   Explanation:

Reference 5 (page ___):

Explanation:

8. Discuss and give a summary of the theme(s) of CIVIL RIGHTS and RACE ISSUES in the book *The Secret Life of Bees*.

ORAL PRESENTATION

You will be asked to give an oral presentation and lead a class discussion about the theme of civil rights/race issues in the book. Use this worksheet as a guide for your presentation.

At the end of your presentation, pose the following questions to your class:

1. Why does Zach love Lily? What characteristics does he see in her that he finds admirable, charming, or loveable?

NOTE: After your classmates offer their ideas and any discussion has subsided, you might note that because Zach sees these qualities in Lily, we also have them pointed out to us, as readers, through him. His view reinforces the hints we have seen that Lily is a very special person.

2. Why does Lily love Zach? What is it about him that she responds to and loves?
3. Is June prejudiced in a racial sense? Why does she treat Lily so poorly at first?
4. Are the Daughters of Mary prejudiced? What is the difference, if any, between being prejudiced and being racially biased?
5. What, if any, progress has been made in civil rights/race issues since the early 1960's? What things promote progress in this area? What things are detrimental to progress?
6. Ask if anyone has anything to add to the discussion of CIVIL RIGHTS/RACE ISSUES in *The Secret Life of Bees* before you close the discussion, and field questions that may be asked.

GROUP WORKSHEET FOR THE THEME OF
COPING
in *The Secret Life of Bees*

List of Group Members (with assigned book chapters to skim for references):

1 ______________________________ Chapters ____________

2 ______________________________ Chapters ____________

3 ______________________________ Chapters ____________

4 ______________________________ Chapters ____________

5 ______________________________ Chapters ____________

6 ______________________________ Chapters ____________

7 ______________________________ Chapters ____________

ASSIGNMENT

Your group's assignment is to examine the topic of COPING throughout *The Secret Life of Bees*.

One group member should read this entire worksheet aloud with the group and lead the group through the work.

After reading through this worksheet, you will each skim through assigned chapters of the book to find references to this topic, jotting down the page number and a few notes about each reference you find.

After you all have completed your skimming and research, you will gather back together to discuss the things you have found and to complete the remainder of this worksheet.

You will then give a short presentation to the class and conduct a short discussion of this aspect of the novel with the class.

PROMPT

The people in *The Secret Life of Bees* have some real issues to cope with. Consider the following:

* Lily has killed her own mother.

* Lily's mother left her.

* The calendar sisters' sister April committed suicide when she was 15.

* May committed suicide, leaving many feeling responsible or as if they could maybe have prevented it.

* June and August were intelligent, educated African-Americans living in the pre-civil rights era South.

* T. Ray's wife was killed, and he was left alone as a single parent.

* Deborah was faced with the prospects of being an unwed mother in the early 1960's. Then she was stuck in a marriage with a man she might not have chosen under different circumstances.
* The Boatwright sisters have a black woman and a white child who have "run away from home" land on their doorstep.
* Rosaleen's life wasn't much different from a slave's life.
* The 1960's were a time of social change and upheaval when the daily news brought to every home unsettling news and pictures of riots as well as acts of violence and destruction.
* Lily and Rosaleen have broken the law and are actually "wanted" criminals.
* August lived for years never knowing what happened to Deborah.

Your assignment is to examine how the people in *The Secret Life of Bees* cope with all of these issues.

RESEARCH

Now do your individual research. Each of you should skim through your chapters of the book to find references to COPING in the text. This will be a little tricky because you have to sort-of read between the lines and recognize the methods and signs of coping. For example, Lily's writing in her journal could be considered a way of coping--as could May's going to the wall, June's throwing tomatoes, and Lily's destroying the honey house, among many, many other things. You just have to think about each person's issues as they come up in the book and see how they act and react given the circumstances. Write down the page number of each reference and a few notes to identify the references.

GROUP DISCUSSION

When you finish finding references in your chapters, get together and discuss what you have found. Tell each other what you found and evaluate your findings. Which references are most relevant and seem most important in the overall picture of the book? Make a special note of these.

Based on the references you found in the text, discuss and answer the following questions:

1. With what does each of the following characters have to cope, and how does each handle his/her situation? Note that some characters have more than one issue to handle.

   Lily

   Deborah

   T. Ray

   August

June

May

Rosaleen

Zach

Neil

Mr. Gaston

2. Some issues in the book are dealt with by action, and other things in the book are dealt with by letting time pass without any particular action. What are some examples of each? What is the value of each of these methods? Consider May's death? Should someone have taken action before she committed suicide? How can you tell when action is needed or not for any particular situation?

3. What role, if any, does Our Lady of Chains play in the theme of coping with issues in *The Secret Life of Bees*?

4. There were many events in the book that could be taken as being negative or "bad things happening." Most of the time when we talk about "issues," we talk about "bad things" that fall into our lives, things we have to cope with. However, look at the issues of each of the characters above and state for each a "good thing" that came about because of the "bad thing" that happened. Make notes above on your list and any additional notes below.

5. Choose five examples of coping with issues from the text, ones you think are the most important, and explain the importance of each.

Reference 1 (page ___):

Explanation:

Reference 2 (page ___):

Explanation:

Reference 3 (page ___):

Explanation:

Reference 4 (page ___):

Explanation:

Reference 5 (page ___):

Explanation:

6. Discuss and give a summary of the theme of COPING WITH ISSUES in the book *The Secret Life of Bees*.

ORAL PRESENTATION

You will be asked to give an oral presentation and lead a class discussion about the theme of "coping" in the book. Use this worksheet as a guide for your presentation.

At the end of your presentation, pose the following questions to your class:

1. If you had been in T. Ray's situation, how would you have felt towards Lily? Assuming you were a good person, how could you have coped with those feelings?
2. Should the calendar sisters have let May go to the wailing wall alone that last time? Was May's death inevitable?
3. Which methods of coping with issues seemed the most effective in the book?
4. After looking at the trials, the issues, the problems faced by the characters in this book–and the positive outcomes caused by living through or working through those issues, what is something positive we can learn from reading this book? [Answer Note: We often say that every cloud has a silver lining, and that is evident in this book. No matter how "bad" something we face seems, we can work through it or live through it knowing that in the end some good will come of it, and we'll be a better person for having coped with the situation.]
5. Ask if anyone has anything to add to the discussion of COPING WITH ISSUES in *The Secret Life of Bees* before you close the discussion, and field questions that may be asked.

GROUP WORKSHEET FOR THE THEME OF FREEDOM
in *The Secret Life of Bees*

List of Group Members (with assigned book chapters to skim for references):

1 ______________________________ Chapters ____________

2 ______________________________ Chapters ____________

3 ______________________________ Chapters ____________

4 ______________________________ Chapters ____________

5 ______________________________ Chapters ____________

6 ______________________________ Chapters ____________

7 ______________________________ Chapters ____________

ASSIGNMENT

Your group's assignment is to examine the topic of FREEDOM throughout *The Secret Life of Bees*.

One group member should read this entire worksheet aloud with the group and lead the group through the work.

After reading through this worksheet, you will each skim through assigned chapters of the book to find references to this topic, jotting down the page number and a few notes about each reference you find.

After you all have completed your skimming and research, you will gather back together to discuss the things you have found and to complete the remainder of this worksheet.

You will then give a short presentation to the class and conduct a short discussion of this aspect of the novel with the class.

PROMPT

What is freedom? How many different kinds of freedom can you list? Make a list here:

Sometimes we take a narrow view of freedom and relate it only to something like slavery or jail, to be free from bondage. Sometimes we think of freedom relating to our country's independence, being free of another country's rules. Freedom also brings to mind things we consider to be our "rights," like the freedom of speech, the freedom to choose our religion (or none), and so on. However, in a broader sense, freedom can mean being free from anything that has a hold on us--like guilt, prejudice, fears, regrets, and so on.

Think about the following characters in the book and make a list of things that keep (or kept) each from being truly "free," considering both external and internal sources.

Lily

T. Ray

June

August

Deborah

May

Rosaleen

Zach

Mr. Gaston

RESEARCH

Now do your individual research. Each of you should skim through your chapters of the book to find references to FREEDOM, as defined by the items you have listed above, in the text. You may have to "read between the lines" to catch some references. Sometimes what a person says or does can be an indication of an issue holding the person back from real freedom. Write down the page number of each reference and a few notes to identify the references.

GROUP DISCUSSION

When you finish finding references in your chapters, get together and discuss what you have found. Tell each other what you found and evaluate your findings. Which references are most relevant and seem most important in the overall picture of the book? Make a special note of these.

Based on the references you found in the text revise or edit the list you made in your initial discussion of each character above.

1. Which character seems to be the most "free"? Justify your answer.

2. August says, "You know, Lily, people can start out one way, and by the time life gets through with them they end up completely different." Being burdened--or freed from burdens--tends to shape our outlook on life and our personalities. Consider these things:

   a. Does Lily change when she leaves home and becomes "free" of T. Ray?

   b. Does Rosaleen change when she is given the freedom to vote?

   c. Does June change when she gives in and frees herself from her resentment of Lily?

d. Does Zach change when he gets freed from jail?

e. Does Deborah change when she becomes burdened with a life she didn't want?

f. Does the hurt June felt from being jilted at the altar change her?

What are some other examples in the novel of people changing because of being burdened with or freed from something? List at least three examples.

1.

2.

3.

3. Sometimes we use the expression "free as a bird." For the purposes of this story, suppose we substitute "bee" for "bird." Are bees really free? What are they free from, if anything? What are they bound by?

4. What did the Black Madonna, Our Lady of Chains, have to with freedom? Brainstorm a list of points that were made regarding freedom using the Black Madonna.

5. "Lily Owens, your jar is open." Discuss this quotation in reference to the theme of freedom in the book.

6. Discuss the presentation of civil rights activities/incidents in relation to the theme of freedom in *The Secret Life of Bees*.

7. Choose five examples of the theme of freedom (based on the definition above under PROMPT) from the text, ones you think are the most important, and explain the importance of each.

   Reference 1 (page ___):

   Explanation:

   Reference 2 (page ___):

   Explanation:

   Reference 3 (page ___):

   Explanation:

   Reference 4 (page ___):

   Explanation:

   Reference 5 (page ___):

   Explanation:

8. Discuss and give a summary of the theme of FREEDOM in the book *The Secret Life of Bees*.

ORAL PRESENTATION

You will be asked to give an oral presentation and lead a class discussion about the theme of freedom in the book. Use this worksheet as a guide for your presentation.

At the end of your presentation, pose the following questions to your class:

1. Based on the ideas presented in *The Secret Life of Bees*, answer the question "What is freedom?".
2. Is freedom real or an illusion? Does it matter? What is important about freedom?
3. Ask if anyone has anything to add to the discussion of FREEDOM in *The Secret Life of Bees* before you close the discussion, and field questions that may be asked.

GROUP WORKSHEET FOR THE THEME OF
CHOOSING WHAT MATTERS
in *The Secret Life of Bees*

List of Group Members (with assigned book chapters to skim for references):

1 ______________________________ Chapters ____________

2 ______________________________ Chapters ____________

3 ______________________________ Chapters ____________

4 ______________________________ Chapters ____________

5 ______________________________ Chapters ____________

6 ______________________________ Chapters ____________

7 ______________________________ Chapters ____________

ASSIGNMENT

Your group's assignment is to examine the topic of CHOOSING WHAT MATTERS throughout *The Secret Life of Bees*.

One group member should read this entire worksheet aloud with the group and lead the group through the work.

After reading through this worksheet, you will each skim through assigned chapters of the book to find references to this topic, jotting down the page number and a few notes about each reference you find.

After you all have completed your skimming and research, you will gather back together to discuss the things you have found and to complete the remainder of this worksheet.

You will then give a short presentation to the class and conduct a short discussion of this aspect of the novel with the class.

PROMPT

August says, "The problem is [people] *know* what matters, but they don't *choose* it." *The Secret Life of Bees* is full of people making choices--good choices, bad choices, or just choices. Take a minute to think about some of the choices the characters in the book made. Who chose what *mattered* as opposed to what was easy or not doing anything? List at lease three examples.

1.

2.

3.

RESEARCH

Now do your individual research. Each of you should skim through your chapters of the book to find references to people's choices in the text. Find places where a character chooses to do something or act in one way as opposed to another. For example, Lily chooses to spring Rosaleen from jail, and Zach chooses to stand with his friends and go to jail. Write down the page number of each reference and a few notes to identify the reference.

GROUP DISCUSSION

When you finish finding references in your chapters, get together and discuss what you have found. Tell each other what you found and evaluate your findings. Which references are most relevant and seem most important in the overall picture of the book? Make a special note of these.

1. Based on the references you found in the text, list the characters who chose "what matters" and tell what they chose.

2. Based on your research in the text, list references to when characters chose to take the "easy" way rather than choosing "what matters."

3. Some characters made decisions that had a profound effect on others in the book. List and briefly describe as many of those incidents as you can find.

What important choices did Deborah make?

What important choices did T. Ray make?

What important choices did Lily make?

What important choices did Rosaleen make?

What important choices did Zach make?

What important choices did August make?

What important choices did June make?

What important choices did May make?

4. From the text choose five references to choices/decisions made, ones you think are the most important, and explain the importance of each.

Reference 1 (page ___):

Explanation:

Reference 2 (page ___):

Explanation:

Reference 3 (page ___):

Explanation:

Reference 4 (page ___):

Explanation:

Reference 5 (page ___):

Explanation:

5. Discuss and give a summary of the theme of CHOOSING WHAT MATTERS in the book *The Secret Life of Bees.*

ORAL PRESENTATION

You will be asked to give an oral presentation and lead a class discussion about the theme of "choosing what matters" in the book. Use this worksheet as a guide for your presentation.

At the end of your presentation, pose the following questions to your class:

1. In *The Secret Life of Bees*, the author shows us many examples of people making decisions about their lives. Based on the examples we are given in the novel, what do you think she is trying to tell us regarding making choices?
2. What does it mean to "choose what matters"?
3. Ask if anyone has anything to add to the discussion of CHOOSING WHAT MATTERS in *The Secret Life of Bees* before you close the discussion, and field questions that may be asked.

LESSONS EIGHTEEN AND NINETEEN

Objectives
To focus on interpretation, critical analysis, and personal responses

Activity 1
Choose the questions from the Extra Writing Assignments/Discussion Questions which seem most appropriate for your students. A class discussion of these questions is most effective if students have been given the opportunity to formulate answers to the questions prior to the discussion. To this end, you may have all students formulate answers to all questions, divide your class into groups and assign one or more questions to each group, or you could assign one question to each student in your class. The option you choose will make a difference in the amount of class time needed for this activity. This LitPlan allows two class meetings for the preparation and discussion of the questions.

Note: The use of graphic organizers may be helpful to students in preparing their answers. Encourage them to use any diagrams or graphics they feel are necessary.

EXTRA WRITING ASSIGNMENTS/DISCUSSION QUESTIONS *The Secret Life of Bees*

Interpretive

1. From what point of view is the story told? How does that affect our perception of the events?
2. What are two major conflicts in the novel? Consider both internal and external conflicts.
3. Is the setting of the novel important to the theme(s)? If so, why? If not, why not?
4. Over what period of time does the actual action of the novel take place?
5. What indications do we have that Deborah is somehow connected to the calendar sisters, even before Lily realizes it?
6. Give two examples of flashback and two examples of foreshadowing used in the novel. What do these techniques add to the novel?

Critical

7. How does Lily's relationship with Rosaleen change throughout the novel? What events bring about these changes?
8. What role do parents, grandparents, and guardians play in this novel? List pairs of "grownups" and younger characters in the novel, and briefly describe the influence each grownup had on the corresponding younger character.
9. Describe two "signature" things about each of these characters: Lily, T. Ray, Rosaleen, August, June, May, Deborah, and Zach.
10. What are T. Ray's good qualities as a parent? What are his worst ones?
11. Describe the relationship among the calendar sisters. How does the relationship affect the plot of the novel?
12. Why are the Daughters of Mary important in the story?
13. What objects belonging to Lily's mother are a part of the story? What do they symbolize?
14. Why might the Daughters of Mary be described as "Orthodox Eclectic"?
15. Compare and contrast August and Rosaleen.
16. What does Our Lady of Chains become to Lily?
17. Compare and contrast Deborah and Lily.
18. What is Neil's purpose in the novel? What would the novel lack without his character?
19. How does Lily change as a result of her experiences with the calendar sisters, and how do they change as a result of their experiences with her?
20. Explain the title of the book: *The Secret Life of Bees.*
21. Why are the bees important in the novel?
22. What purpose do the epigraphs serve in the novel? Would the novel have been as good without them? Explain your answer.
23. Compare and contrast Rosaleen's relationship with May to June's relationship with May.
24. The author could have made May be any kind of a person at all. Why did she choose to make May the way she did? What did May add to the novel?
25. Does T. Ray love Lily? Support your answer.
26. What are Rosaleen's best qualities? Her worst?

27. Why do Rosaleen and May get along so well?
28. What comments about religion does the author make through the events with Our Lady of Chains and the Daughters of Mary?
29. The issue of "mother" and motherhood is a big part of the book. What mothers and mother figures are present in the book? What points does the author make about mothers and motherhood? Explain.
30. There are many references to praying and religion in the book. What points does the author make about religion through the events in the book? Explain fully.
31. What is The Secret Life of Bees ultimately about? What is or are the main idea(s)we are supposed to get from reading it? Support your answer with examples from the text.
32. What comments does the author make about race and race relations through the events of the book? Support your answer.
33. Compare and contrast August and June.
34. Compare and contrast Neil and Zach.
35. The truth, in the end, was that Lily did kill her mother by accident when she was as mall child. This event is very much a part of the whole story. Why? What does it have to do with the theme(s) of the story?
36. Discuss the theme of "freedom" as it relates to the novel.
37. Discuss the theme of wisdom in the novel. To whom do people go to for advice and help? Who is wise, and who is not? Explain.
38. People get angry in this book. Lily has issues with anger, as do Zach and T. Ray. Explain what causes each of these characters to be deeply angry. Does being angry help their situations? When do they make their best decisions, when they are angry--or not?
39. Discuss how the author symbolically uses water in the novel. Give at least three examples and explain each.

<u>Critical/Personal Response</u>

40. Why do you think Lily waits to talk to August even after she learns about her mother's history with the calendar sisters?
41. Do you think Lily is a "typical" teenager? In what ways is she "typical," and in what ways is she unusual or extraordinary?
42. Who is your favorite character in The Secret Life of Bees? Why? Find a passage from the novel that demonstrates the quality you most admire in that character.
43. Discuss two events from the novel that give us a taste of real life in the south in the early 1960's.
44. Was Lily right to run away with Rosaleen? Did she do the right thing? Support your answer.
45. Is it believable that the calendar sisters would take in Lily and Rosaleen? Why or why not?
46. August seems to be a very special person. What are her best qualities? Does she have any negative traits? If so, what are they?
47. Discuss the theme of forgiveness in the novel.
48. Who was responsible for Deborah's death? Justify your answer.

<u>Personal Response</u>

49. August gives Lily some of her mother's items toward the end of the novel. Do you own any items that are special to you because they once belonged to someone else? What are they, and why are they special?

50. Our Lady of Chains and the Daughters of Mary figure prominently in this novel. What ceremonies exist in your own culture and family? List and explain any religious and non-religious examples.
51. Which character from the novel would you most like to meet in person and become friends with? Why?
52. What else would you like to know about any of the characters in the novel after the end of the book?
53. What is your favorite scene, moment, or line from the novel?
54. Do you think everyone should have a "wailing wall"? Why or why not? Would you like to have one?

LESSON TWENTY

Objectives
To review the vocabulary work done in this unit

Activity
Choose one (or more) of the vocabulary review activities listed below and spend your class time as directed. Some of the materials for these review activities are located in the vocabulary resource materials section of this LitPlan.

VOCABULARY REVIEW ACTIVITIES

1. Divide your class into two teams and have an old-fashioned spelling or definition bee.

2. Give each of your students (or students in groups of two, three or four) a *Secret Life of Bees* Vocabulary Word Search Puzzle. The person (group) to find all of the vocabulary words in the puzzle first wins.

3. Give students a *Secret Life of Bees* Vocabulary Word Search Puzzle without the word list. The person or group to find the most vocabulary words in the puzzle wins.

4. Use a *Secret Life of Bees* Vocabulary Crossword Puzzle. Put the puzzle onto a transparency on the overhead projector (so everyone can see it), and do the puzzle together as a class.

5. Give students a *Secret Life of Bees* Vocabulary Matching Worksheet to do.

6. Divide your class into two teams. Use *Secret Life of Bees* vocabulary words with their letters jumbled as a word list. Student 1 from Team A faces off against Student 1 from Team B. You write the first jumbled word on the board. The first student (1A or 1B) to unscramble the word wins the chance for his/her team to score points. If 1A wins the jumble, go to student 2A and give him/her a definition. He/she must give you the correct spelling of the vocabulary word which fits that definition. If he/she does, Team A scores a point, and you give student 3A a definition for which you expect a correctly spelled matching vocabulary word. Continue giving Team A definitions until some team member makes an incorrect response. An incorrect response sends the game back to the jumbled-word face off, this time with students 2A and 2B. Instead of repeating giving definitions to the first few students of each team, continue with the student after the one who gave the last incorrect response on the team. For example, if Team B wins the jumbled-word face-off, and student 5B gave the last incorrect answer for Team B, you would start this round of definition questions with student 6B, and so on. The team with the most points wins!

7. Have students write a story in which they correctly use as many vocabulary words as possible. Have students read their compositions orally! Post the most original compositions on your bulletin board!

LESSON TWENTY-ONE

Objectives
To review the main events and idea in *The Secret Life of Bees*

Activity
Choose one of the review games/activities suggested in this unit and spend your class time as directed there.

REVIEW GAMES/ACTIVITIES

1. Ask the class to make up a unit test for *The Secret Life of Bees.* The test should have 4 sections: matching, true/false, short answer, and essay. Students may use 1/2 period to make the test and then swap papers and use the other 1/2 class period to take a test a classmate has devised. (open book) You may want to use the unit test included in this packet or take questions from the students' unit tests to formulate your own test.

2. Take 1/2 period for students to make up true and false questions (including the answers). Collect the papers and divide the class into two teams. Draw a big tic-tac-toe board on the chalk board. Make one team X and one team O. Ask questions to each side, giving each student one turn. If the question is answered correctly, that students' team's letter (X or O) is placed in the box. If the answer is incorrect, no letter is placed in the box. The object is to get three in a row like tic-tac-toe. You may want to keep track of the number of games won for each team.

3. Take 1/2 period for students to make up questions (true/false and short answer). Collect the questions. Divide the class into two teams. You'll alternate asking questions to individual members of teams A & B (like in a spelling bee). The question keeps going from A to B until it is correctly answered, then a new question is asked. A correct answer does not allow the team to get another question. Correct answers are +2 points; incorrect answers are -1 point.

4. Have students pair up and quiz each other from their study guides and class notes.

5. Give students a *Secret Life of Bees* crossword puzzle to complete.

6. Play What's My Line?. This is similar to the old television show. Students assume the roles of different characters from the novel. One student gives clues to the class, or to a panel of contestants. The contestants try to guess the identity of the guest. Students may enjoy assisting you in creating rules and procedures for the game.

7. Divide your class into two teams. Use the *Secret Life of Bees* words with the letters jumbled as a word list. Student 1 from Team A faces off against Student 1 from Team B. You write the first jumbled word on the board. The first student (1A or 1B) to unscramble the word wins the chance for his/her team to score points. If 1A wins the jumble, go to student 2A and give him/her a clue. He/she must give you the correct word which matches that clue. If he/she does, Team A scores a point, and you give student 3A a clue for which you expect another correct response. Continue giving Team A clues until some team member makes an incorrect response. An incorrect response sends the game back to the jumbled-word face off, this time with students 2A and 2B. Instead of repeating giving clues to the first few students of each team, continue with the student after the one who gave the last incorrect response on the team. For example, if Team B wins the jumbled-word face-off, and student 5B gave the last incorrect answer for Team B, you would start this round of clue questions with student 6B, and so on. The team with the most points wins!

8. Play Jeopardy. Divide the class into two groups. Assign each group a category or book from

the novel and have them devise answers for that category. Play the game according to the television show procedures.

9. Play Drawing in the Details. This is similar to Pictionary. Divide students into teams. A student from one team draws a scene from the novel. (You may want to specify the Book or section.) Drawings should be kept simple, to keep the pace lively. Students in the opposing team locate the scene in their books and read it aloud. If they are incorrect, the illustrator's team has a chance to guess. Involve students in setting up a scoring system and any other necessary rules.

LESSON TWENTY-TWO

Objectives
To assess students' understanding of the events and ideas presented through *The Secret Life of Bees*

Activity
Distribute the unit tests, give students ample time to complete them, and collect the tests when students finish. Remember to collect assigned books prior to the end of the class period.

NOTE: There are 5 different unit tests included in the LitPlan Teacher Pack. Two are short answer, two are multiple choice. There is one advanced short answer test. The answers to the advanced short answer test will be based on the discussions you have had during class and should be graded accordingly. You should choose the tests and/or test parts which best suit your needs. Matching and short answer tests have answer keys. For essay type questions, grade according to your own criteria based on class discussions and the level of your students. Also, you will need to choose vocabulary words to read orally for the vocabulary section of the short answer tests.

UNIT TESTS

The Secret Life of Bees Short Answer Unit Test 1

I. Matching

____ 1.	LILY	A.	Lily calls T. Ray from his office.
____ 2.	ROSALEEN	B.	He wants to marry June.
____ 3.	RAY	C.	Author
____ 4.	DEBORAH	D.	Lily helped her escape.
____ 5.	VIRGINIA	E.	Compassionate and sensible bee-keeper
____ 6.	JOHNSON	F.	Lily's father; T. ___
____ 7.	ORCHARD	G.	Lily's place of peace and comfort
____ 8.	GASTON	H.	He tells Lily to hush when Rosaleen is struck with the flashlight.
____ 9.	OWENS	I.	Lily says he is one-third friend, one-third brother, one-third bee partner, & one-third boyfriend.
____ 10.	MAY	J.	She ran away from home.
____ 11.	APRIL	K.	She lacks built-in protection around her heart.
____ 12.	NEIL	L.	She committed suicide at age 15.
____ 13.	ZACH	M.	Boatwrights' grandmother: Big ___
____ 14.	FORREST	N.	Lily's mother
____ 15.	FONTANEL	O.	Lily's mother's maiden name
____ 16.	BECCA	P.	Lily's last name
____ 17.	MAMA	Q.	Clayton Forrest's daughter
____ 18.	AUGUST	R.	Musician who resents Lily
____ 19.	JUNE	S.	Home state of Deborah and August
____ 20.	KIDD	T.	This President signed the Civil Rights Act into law.

II. Short Answer

1. What happened to Lily's mother?

2. The morning after she is punished for being in the orchard, Lily wakes up late. T. Ray yells at her for not going to work at the peach stand on time. What does Lily understand after T. Ray tells her, "As long as you're under my roof, you'll do what I say!"?

3. After T. Ray gets Lily out of jail, they have a fight. What does T. Ray say to Lily that "would sink [her] forever"?

4. What first lets Lily know she has some prejudice buried inside herself?

5. What is the "wailing wall"?

6. Who are The Daughters of Mary?

7. What does August say is the whole problem with people?

8. What happens when Zach and Lily ride to town to get a new radiator hose?

9. What is Mary Day?

10. How does having her mother's things and knowing the whole story affect Lily? What does she do?

11. How does T. Ray find Lily?

12. Lily runs after T. Ray as he leaves, yelling for him to stop. What does she ask him, and what is his response?

III. Composition

1. Describe two "signature" things about each of these characters: Lily, T. Ray, Rosaleen, August, June, May, Deborah, and Zach.

2. Why are the bees important in the novel?

IV. Vocabulary

A. Write the vocabulary words you are given. After writing them down, go back and write in their definitions.

Word	Definition
1	
2	
3	
4	
5	
6	
7	
8	
9	
10	

The Secret Life of Bees Short Answer Unit Test 1 Answer Key

I. Matching

Answer	Term		Description
J	1. LILY	A.	Lily calls T. Ray from his office.
D	2. ROSALEEN	B.	He wants to marry June.
F	3. RAY	C.	Author
N	4. DEBORAH	D.	Lily helped her escape.
S	5. VIRGINIA	E.	Compassionate and sensible bee-keeper
T	6. JOHNSON	F.	Lily's father; T. ___
G	7. ORCHARD	G.	Lily's place of peace and comfort
H	8. GASTON	H.	He tells Lily to hush when Rosaleen is struck with the flashlight.
P	9. OWENS	I.	Lily says he is one-third friend, one-third brother, one-third bee partner, & one-third boyfriend.
K	10. MAY	J.	She ran away from home.
L	11. APRIL	K.	She lacks built-in protection around her heart.
B	12. NEIL	L.	She committed suicide at age 15.
I	13. ZACH	M.	Boatwrights' grandmother: Big ___
A	14. FORREST	N.	Lily's mother
O	15. FONTANEL	O.	Lily's mother's maiden name
Q	16. BECCA	P.	Lily's last name
M	17. MAMA	Q.	Clayton Forrest's daughter
E	18. AUGUST	R.	Musician who resents Lily
R	19. JUNE	S.	Home state of Deborah and August
C	20. KIDD	T.	This President signed the Civil Rights Act into law.

II. Short Answer

1. What happened to Lily's mother?
When she was four years old, Lily accidently shot and killed her mother.

2. The morning after she is punished for being in the orchard, Lily wakes up late. T. Ray yells at her for not going to work at the peach stand on time. What does Lily understand after T. Ray tells her, "As long as you're under my roof, you'll do what I say!"?
Lily understands that "a new rooftop would do wonders" for her. She understands that she needs to leave home.

3. After T. Ray gets Lily out of jail, they have a fight. What does T. Ray say to Lily that "would sink [her] forever"?
He says, ". . . your sorry mother ran off and left you. The day she died, she'd come back to get her things, that's all. You can hate me all you want, but she's *the one who left you."*

4. What first lets Lily know she has some prejudice buried inside herself?
". . . all I could think was August is so intelligent, so cultured*, and I was surprised by this. That's what let me know I had some prejudice buried inside me."*

5. What is the "wailing wall"?
It is a wall in Jerusalem where the Jewish people go to mourn. They write their prayers on scraps of paper and tuck them into the wall. June and August came up with the idea of a wailing wall to help May deal with her issues.

6. Who are The Daughters of Mary?
They are a group of women (and one man) who meet at the Boatwrights' house to honor and pray to Mary. They were Queenie, Violet, Lunelle, Mabelee, Cressie, Sugar-Girl, and Otis.

7. What does August say is the whole problem with people?
They know *what matters, but they don't* choose *it.*

8. What happens when Zach and Lily ride to town to get a new radiator hose?
Some of Zach's friends get into an incident with white men who were waiting for Jack Palance outside the movie theater. One of the boys throws a bottle at one of the white men and gives him a bloody nose. Zach stands with the boys, and they are all arrested.

9. What is Mary Day?
On the Feast of the Assumption (Mary's feast day), the Daughters of Mary have a big (two-day) event in which they celebrate the feast day for Mary, have a special remembrance for Our Lady of Chains, and give thanks for the honey crop.

10. How does having her mother's things and knowing the whole story affect Lily? What does she do?
Lily pulls away into herself, wanting to be alone. She spends a period of time thinking, trying not to think, and grieving.

11. How does T. Ray find Lily?
His phone bill had a collect call from Mr. Clayton Forrest's office. He goes to the office and finds out from the secretary where to find Lily.

12. Lily runs after T. Ray as he leaves, yelling for him to stop. What does she ask him, and what is his response?
Lily asks him for the truth about her mother's death, if she really did accidentally kill her mother. T. Ray softens and confesses that she really did do it without meaning to.

IV. Vocabulary

A. Write the vocabulary words you are given. After writing them down, go back and write in their definitions.

Word	Definition
1	
2	
3	
4	
5	
6	
7	
8	
9	
10	

Select the vocabulary words for Short Answer Test 1

The Secret Life of Bees Short Answer Unit Test 2

I. Matching

____ 1.	BUGS	A.	Zach's gift to Lily
____ 2.	MADONNA	B.	Our Lady of ___
____ 3.	PEACH	C.	Lily's place of peace and comfort
____ 4.	BRACELET	D.	Birthday present Lily wants: charm ___
____ 5.	ORCHARD	E.	Bee yard etiquette says if you are angry you should do this.
____ 6.	GRITS	F.	Place where Lily worked: ___ stand
____ 7.	FAN	G.	Frogmore ___ General Store
____ 8.	STEW	H.	The black ___ picture led Lily to August.
____ 9.	WHISTLE	I.	The most important item in the hat box
____ 10.	LOVE	J.	August covered them with black cloths after May died.
____ 11.	WAILING	K.	Bee yard etiquette says you should send the bees this.
____ 12.	CHAINS	L.	June throws these at Neil.
____ 13.	TOMATOES	M.	Object Lily wears that holds T. Ray's attention
____ 14.	HIVES	N.	May left one for August and June.
____ 15.	NOTE	O.	June and Lily wrestle over it.
____ 16.	CALENDAR	P.	Deborah was a lunatic when it came to saving these.
____ 17.	PICTURE	Q.	Nickname for the Boatwrights: ___ sisters
____ 18.	SPRINKLER	R.	The stone wall is May's ___ wall.
____ 19.	NOTEBOOK	S.	Item Rosaleen steals from the church
____ 20.	PIN	T.	T. Ray makes Lily kneel on these.

II. Short Answer

1. Before Lily went into first grade, T. Ray came to the peach stand to tell her something. What did he want to tell her? Why?

2. For what is Rosaleen arrested?

3. After Lily pours the tear drop out of the bottom of the bee jar, she has a "true religious moment" and hears a voice say something. What does the voice say?

4. Lily sees something in the Frogmore Stew General Store and Restaurant that shocks her. What does she see?

5. August tells Lily how May is special. What does she say?

6. Lily tells Zach, "You've got to hear of these things before you can imagine them." What is Zach's response?

7. What critical piece of information does May tell Lily?

8. What happens to May after she goes to the wailing wall for the last time?

9. What brings Lily the most cause for gladness while the Daughters of Mary are holding vigil for May?

10. What does August tell Lily that she always wants Lily to remember?

11. What happens in the afternoon after August had taken Lily to see the queenless colony?

12. What is the closing image of the novel?

III. Quotations: Explain the importance and meaning of the following quotations:

1. "You ain't touching that chick." (11)

2. "As long as you're under my roof, you'll do what I say!" (26)

3. "I can't say what men riled up like that will do." (35)

4. If only she could get some manners. (75)

5. "Oh, yes. Deborah Fontanel. She stayed out there in the honey house. She was the sweetest thing." (173)

6. "You know, Lily, people can start out one way, and by the time life gets through with them they end up completely different." (248)

7. "Oh, Lily. Why would I go and hurt you with something like that?" (265)

8. "Regrets don't help anything, you know that." (280)

9. "Our Lady is not some magical being out there somewhere, like a fairy godmother. She's not the statue in the parlor. She's something inside of you. Do you understand what I'm telling you?" (288)

IV. Vocabulary

A. Write the vocabulary words you are given. After writing them down, go back and write in their definitions.

Word	Definition
1	
2	
3	
4	
5	
6	
7	
8	
9	
10	

The Secret Life of Bees Short Answer Unit Test 2 Answer Key

I. Matching

P	1. BUGS	A.	Zach's gift to Lily
H	2. MADONNA	B.	Our Lady of ___
F	3. PEACH	C.	Lily's place of peace and comfort
D	4. BRACELET	D.	Birthday present Lily wants: charm ___
C	5. ORCHARD	E.	Bee yard etiquette says if you are angry you should do this.
T	6. GRITS	F.	Place where Lily worked: ___ stand
S	7. FAN	G.	Frogmore ___ General Store
G	8. STEW	H.	The black ___ picture led Lily to August.
E	9. WHISTLE	I.	The most important item in the hat box
K	10. LOVE	J.	August covered them with black cloths after May died.
R	11. WAILING	K.	Bee yard etiquette says you should send the bees this.
B	12. CHAINS	L.	June throws these at Neil.
L	13. TOMATOES	M.	Object Lily wears that holds T. Ray's attention
J	14. HIVES	N.	May left one for August and June.
N	15. NOTE	O.	June and Lily wrestle over it.
Q	16. CALENDAR	P.	Deborah was a lunatic when it came to saving these.
I	17. PICTURE	Q.	Nickname for the Boatwrights: ___ sisters
O	18. SPRINKLER	R.	The stone wall is May's ___ wall.
A	19. NOTEBOOK	S.	Item Rosaleen steals from the church
M	20. PIN	T.	T. Ray makes Lily kneel on these.

II. Short Answer

1. Before Lily went into first grade, T. Ray came to the peach stand to tell her something. What did he want to tell her? Why?
   He wanted to tell her how her mother died so she wouldn't hear it from other people at school.
2. For what is Rosaleen arrested?
   She is arrested for assault, theft, and disturbing the peace.
3. After Lily pours the tear drop out of the bottom of the bee jar, she has a "true religious moment" and hears a voice say something. What does the voice say?
   It says, "Lily Melissa Owens, your jar is open."
4. Lily sees something in the Frogmore Stew General Store and Restaurant that shocks her. What does she see?
   She sees a picture of a black Madonna that is exactly the same as her mother's.
5. August tells Lily how May is special. What does she say?
   ". . . It's like we have built-in protection around our hearts that keeps the pain from overwhelming us. But May--she doesn't have that. Everything just comes to her--all the suffering out there--and she feels as if it's happening to her. She can't tell the difference."
6. Lily tells Zach, "You've got to hear of these things before you can imagine them." What is Zach's response?
   He says, "You've gotta imagine what's never been."
7. What critical piece of information does May tell Lily?
   May tells Lily that Deborah Fontanel stayed out in the honey house and was "the sweetest thing."
8. What happens to May after she goes to the wailing wall for the last time?
   She goes to the river, pulls a rock onto herself, and drowns herself in the river.
9. What brings Lily the most cause for gladness while the Daughters of Mary are holding vigil for May?
   Sugar-Girl makes a joke about white people, and no one there even thinks about Lily's being white. It is like she "was truly one of them."
10. What does August tell Lily that she always wants Lily to remember?
    She says, "Our Lady is not some magical being out there somewhere, like a fairy godmother. She's not the statue in the parlor. She's something inside *you. . . . You have to find a mother inside of yourself. . . . She's the power inside you. . . . not only the power inside you but the love. And when you get down to it, Lily, that's the only purpose grand enough for a human life. Not just to love--but to* persist *in love. . . . This Mary I'm talking about sits in your heart all day long, saying, 'Lily, you are my everlasting home. Don't you ever be afraid. I am enough. We are enough.'"*
11. What happens in the afternoon after August had taken Lily to see the queenless colony?
    T. Ray comes to the Boatwrights' house to take Lily home.
12. What is the closing image of the novel?
    The women in Lily's life are standing strongly behind her--her mothers.

IV. Vocabulary

A. Write the vocabulary words you are given. After writing them down, go back and write in their definitions.

Word	Definition
1	
2	
3	
4	
5	
6	
7	
8	
9	
10	

Select the vocabulary words for Short Answer Test 2

The Secret Life of Bees Advanced Short Answer Unit Test

I. Matching

____	1.	LILY	A.	He wants to marry June.
____	2.	ROSALEEN	B.	Lily calls T. Ray from his office.
____	3.	RAY	C.	Written on back of the black madonna picture: ___ S.C.
____	4.	DEBORAH	D.	Lily's father; T. ___
____	5.	VIRGINIA	E.	Lily says he is one-third friend, one-third brother, one-third bee partner, & one-third boyfriend.
____	6.	MADONNA	F.	Lily's last name
____	7.	GASTON	G.	Compassionate and sensible bee-keeper
____	8.	OWENS	H.	She ran away from home.
____	9.	TIBURON	I.	She lacks built-in protection around her heart.
____	10.	BOATWRIGHT	J.	Clayton Forrest's daughter
____	11.	MAY	K.	In every picture, he had a big white lily for Mary.
____	12.	APRIL	L.	She committed suicide at age 15.
____	13.	NEIL	M.	The black ___ picture led Lily to August.
____	14.	ZACH	N.	He tells Lily to hush when Rosaleen is struck with the flashlight.
____	15.	FORREST	O.	Lily's mother's maiden name
____	16.	FONTANEL	P.	Lily helped her escape.
____	17.	GABRIEL	Q.	Musician who resents Lily
____	18.	BECCA	R.	Lily's mother
____	19.	AUGUST	S.	Home state of Deborah and August
____	20.	JUNE	T.	August's last name

II. Short Answer

1. From what point of view is the story told? How does that affect our perception of the events?

2. What are two major conflicts in the novel? Discuss each.

3. Describe two "signature" things about each of these characters: Lily, T. Ray, Rosaleen, August, June, May, Deborah, and Zach.

4. Why are the Daughters of Mary important in the story?

5. Compare and contrast Deborah and Lily.

6. Why are the bees important in the novel?

7. Does T. Ray love Lily? Support your answer.

8. Was Lily right to run away with Rosaleen? Did she do the right thing? Support your answer.

9. The truth, in the end, was that Lily *did* kill her mother by accident when she was a small child. This event is very much a part of the whole story. Why? What does it have to do with the theme(s) of the story?

10. Discuss how the author symbolically uses water in the novel. Give at least three examples and explain each.

III. Composition

1. What is *The Secret Life of Bees* ultimately about? What is or are the main idea(s) we are supposed to get from reading it? Support your answer with examples from the text.

IV. Quotations: Explain the importance and meaning of the following quotations:

1. "The day she died, she'd come back to get her things, that's all. You can hate me all you want, but she's the one who left you." (39)

2. But I had such a moment right then, standing in my own ordinary room. I heard a voice say, *Lily Melissa Owens, your jar is open.* (41)

3. She stopped right in the middle of the song, and I was left in the silence with my hand stretched out. (111)

4. "You've gotta imagine what's never been." (121)

5. Rosaleen reminded me of the stature of Our Lady in the parlor, and I thought, *If August is the red heart on Mary's chest, Rosaleen is the fist*. (182)

6. "It is only a reenactment," August had said. "To help us remember. Remembering is everything." Still, the whole idea wrapped me in sadness. I hated remembering. (228)

7. Knowing can be a curse on a person's life. I'd traded a pack of lies for a pack of truth, and I didn't know which one was heavier. (255)

8. There is nothing perfect. . . . There is only life. (256)

9. "Regrets don't help anything, you know that." (280)

10. "Our Lady is not some magical being out there somewhere, like a fairy godmother. She's not the statue in the parlor. She's something inside of you. Do you understand what I'm telling you?" (288)

11. I remember the sight of them standing there waiting. All these women, all this love, waiting. (299)

V. Vocabulary

A. Write the vocabulary words you are given. After writing them down, go back and write in their definitions.

Word	Definition
1	
2	
3	
4	
5	
6	
7	
8	
9	
10	

The Secret Life of Bees Advanced Short Answer Unit Test Answer Key

I. Matching

H	1. LILY	A.	He wants to marry June.
P	2. ROSALEEN	B.	Lily calls T. Ray from his office.
D	3. RAY	C.	Written on back of the black madonna picture: ___ S.C.
R	4. DEBORAH	D.	Lily's father; T. ___
S	5. VIRGINIA	E.	Lily says he is one-third friend, one-third brother, one-third bee partner, & one-third boyfriend.
M	6. MADONNA	F.	Lily's last name
N	7. GASTON	G.	Compassionate and sensible bee-keeper
F	8. OWENS	H.	She ran away from home.
C	9. TIBURON	I.	She lacks built-in protection around her heart.
T	10. BOATWRIGHT	J.	Clayton Forrest's daughter
I	11. MAY	K.	In every picture, he had a big white lily for Mary.
L	12. APRIL	L.	She committed suicide at age 15.
A	13. NEIL	M.	The black ___ picture led Lily to August.
E	14. ZACH	N.	He tells Lily to hush when Rosaleen is struck with the flashlight.
B	15. FORREST	O.	Lily's mother's maiden name
O	16. FONTANEL	P.	Lily helped her escape.
K	17. GABRIEL	Q.	Musician who resents Lily
J	18. BECCA	R.	Lily's mother
G	19. AUGUST	S.	Home state of Deborah and August
Q	20. JUNE	T.	August's last name

IV. Vocabulary

A. Write the vocabulary words you are given. After writing them down, go back and write in their definitions.

Word	Definition
1	
2	
3	
4	
5	
6	
7	
8	
9	
10	

Select the vocabulary words for Advanced Short Answer Test

The Secret Life of Bees Multiple Choice Unit Test 1

I. Matching

____ 1.	LILY	A.	Lily yells this, and T. Ray is jolted back to reality.
____ 2.	ROSALEEN	B.	Lily's place of peace and comfort
____ 3.	RAY	C.	Without her, the colony of bees will die.
____ 4.	DEBORAH	D.	Lily's mother's maiden name
____ 5.	VIRGINIA	E.	Lily's last name
____ 6.	ORCHARD	F.	August's last name
____ 7.	OWENS	G.	She ran away from home.
____ 8.	TIBURON	H.	Lily calls T. Ray from his office.
____ 9.	BOATWRIGHT	I.	Compassionate and sensible bee-keeper
____ 10.	STREAM	J.	Place where Lily and Rosaleen reunite
____ 11.	LOVE	K.	Boatwrights' grandmother: Big ___
____ 12.	WAILING	L.	Bee yard etiquette says you should send the bees this.
____ 13.	ZACH	M.	Written on back of the black Madonna picture: ___ S.C.
____ 14.	FORREST	N.	Home state of Deborah and August
____ 15.	FONTANEL	O.	Lily says he is one-third friend, one-third brother, one-third bee partner, & one-third boyfriend.
____ 16.	DADDY	P.	Lily's mother
____ 17.	MAMA	Q.	Lily helped her escape.
____ 18.	QUEEN	R.	The stone wall is May's ___ wall.
____ 19.	AUGUST	S.	Musician who resents Lily
____ 20.	JUNE	T.	Lily's father; T. ___

II. Multiple Choice

1. What does Lily think will give her a "real chance" to learn how to be a beautiful, fashionable girl?
   A. A new television show
   B. Charm school
   C. A fashion magazine subscription
   D. A new mother

2. What happens when Zach and Lily ride to town to get a new radiator hose?
   A. Zach gets Jack Palance's autograph.
   B. Zach kisses Lily.
   C. Some white men beat up Zach.
   D. Zach is arrested.

3. What is August's reply when Lily asks if she believes putting black cloths over the hives will help May get to heaven?
   A. August says, "Putting black cloths on the hives is for us. I do it to remind us that life gives way into death, and then death turns around and gives way into life."
   B. August says, "No, I don't. But I do believe in tradition, that traditions help us get through times like these. So I put on the cloths."
   C. August smiles and says, "No, child, I know May has already gone to heaven. The bees know when we're upset, though, and they get upset, too. Covering the hives helps to keep them calmer and happier."
   D. August says, "It isn't that the hives are covered, it's the covering of the hives that helps--helps us, not May. Keeping busy distracts us a little and gives us time to accept the loss without being totally focussed on it."

4. What important message is in May's note to August and June?
   A. "Our Lady of Chains told me this is the best thing for me. I have faith."
   B. "It's my time to die, and it's your time to live. Don't mess it up."
   C. "I don't want to be a burden to you anymore. The world is too sad of a place for me to be. Be glad I have gone on."
   D. "This is nobody's fault. It just is. I no longer need a wailing wall."

5. What promise does Zach make to Lily?
   A. He says, ". . . one day, after I've gone away and become somebody, I'm gonna find you, and we'll be together then."
   B. He says, ". . . and there will come a time when the world will understand that, black or white, we are all human with human hearts and desires. You will always be in my heart, always be my true love, always be my best friend."
   C. He says, ". . . just like the honey bee returns home to the hive, I'll come back to you."
   D. He says, ". . . and I won't ever let them make you go back to T. Ray."

6. Identify Tica Tee.
   A. Tica Tee was Lily's mother's imaginary friend.
   B. Tica Tee was Lily's mother's favorite doll.
   C. Tica Tee was Deborah's nickname for August.
   D. Tica Tee is Sugar-Girl's daughter.

7. Why do the Daughters of Mary rub honey all over Our Lady?
   A. To preserve her
   B. To symbolize their sins sticking to her
   C. To keep her color black
   D. As an offering for the next bee harvest

8. Why is the photograph in the hat box so important?
   A. The look on her mother's face shows Lily that her mother loved her.
   B. It is the only picture of Lily's mother and grandmother together.
   C. On the back it says, "My Lovely Lily" in Deborah's own handwriting, a name of endearment proving Lily's mother loved her.
   D. It shows Deborah and T. Ray, happy on their wedding day, proving that Deborah and T. Ray really were happy together at least at first.

9. What does August tell Lily that she always wants Lily to remember?
   A. She says, "Never forget Our Lady."
   B. She says, "Our Lady is . . . something *inside* you.
   C. She says, "Our Lady is taking care of your mother--and May--and she is waiting, in time, to take care of you."
   D. She says, "You will always have a friend in me--and in Our Lady. She will always give you strength when you are in need, and I shall be here for you as long as I live."

10. What is the result of Lily and June's fighting over the water sprinkler?
   A. They both end up laughing, and June hugs Lily.
   B. Lily gets a bad cut over her left eye, which has to be bandaged.
   C. June falls down in the slippery grass, and Lily laughs at her.
   D. Lily's face gets covered in mud, and June makes a curt, racial remark.

11. What does August say is the whole problem with people?
   A. They *think* they are doing good things, but what they choose to do is usually *not* good.
   B. They *know* what matters, but they don't *choose* it.
   C. People are too blinded by their own prejudices to choose wisely.
   D. They are too stupid to see just how prejudiced they are.

12. Which is NOT a "scrap of information" Lily knows about her mother?
   A. She was an only child.
   B. She used to be a waitress.
   C. She was from Virginia.
   D. She was a lunatic when it came to saving bugs.

13. The morning after she is punished for being in the orchard, Lily wakes up late. T. Ray yells at her for not going to work at the peach stand on time. What does Lily understand after T. Ray tells her, "As long as you're under my roof, you'll do what I say!"?
   A. She understands why her mother left.
   B. She understands that T. Ray is a tyrant.
   C. She understands that she needs to leave home.
   D. She understands that T. Ray loves her.

14. After Lily pours the tear drop out of the bottom of the bee jar, she has a "true religious moment" and hears a voice say something. What does the voice say?
   A. It says, "Lily Melissa Owens, your jar is open."
   B. It says, "Lily Melissa Owens, that man is holding you back."
   C. It says, "Lily Melissa Owens, it's now or never."
   D. It says, "Lily Melissa Owens, pray for forgiveness."

15. What first lets Lily know she has some prejudice buried inside herself?
    A. She is surprised that the sisters keep such a neat, clean house.
    B. She is surprised that the sisters speak so well.
    C. She is surprised that the food at dinner is just ordinary food.
    D. She is surprised that August is so cultured and intelligent.

16. For what special help did Lily pray to Mary?
    A. ". . . I asked her to make August like me and want to keep me. I asked this daily. . . . "
    B. ". . . I asked her to draw a curtain around the pink house so no one would ever find us. I asked this daily. . . . "
    C. ". . . I asked her to forgive me. I asked this daily. . . . "
    D. ". . . I asked her to help T. Ray learn to be less mean and more forgiving. I asked this daily. . . . "

17. Which of these events does NOT happen when Lily goes to touch the heart of Our Lady of Chains?
    A. Lily faints.
    B. June stops playing music.
    C. The Daughters of Mary collectively and spontaneously gasp.
    D. Lily freezes with her arm outstretched towards Mary.

18. What surprises Zach about Lily?
    A. She is younger than he thought.
    B. She is older than he thought.
    C. She looks so much like her mother.
    D. She is white.

19. Which of the statements below is NOT something Lily learns from August while they are pasting labels on the jars of honey?
    A. She learns how August came to own the house and bee business.
    B. She learns how and why the black Madonna came to be on the jar labels.
    C. She learns that August lived in Richmond but came here to visit her grandmother.
    D. She learns that August was once married, but her husband died.

20. What declaration does Lily make to T. Ray?

A. She tells him she will not go back with him.

B. She tells him he has lost.

C. She tells him her mother is dead, and there is nothing either of them can do about that fact.

D. She tells him she will never love him.

III. Composition

1. What comments does the author make about race and race relations through the events of the book? Support your answer.

2. Discuss the theme of forgiveness in the novel.

IV. Vocabulary

____ 1.	SPECTACLE	A.	Place of religious seclusion and meditation
____ 2.	LURING	B.	Device encircling the necks of a pair of oxen, mules, or other draft animals walking in a team; a restrictive or repressive force
____ 3.	RILED	C.	An all-night event spent watching, praying, or guarding
____ 4.	BRAZEN	D.	Bold
____ 5.	PIOUS	E.	Completely unaware
____ 6.	ELUSIVE	F.	Offering something tempting in order to persuade
____ 7.	SALVATION	G.	Undeserving of respect
____ 8.	INDIGNATION	H.	Continually; always; without end
____ 9.	VIGILANTE	I.	Gave up something willingly
____ 10.	INGENIOUS	J.	Anger due to injustice or unreasonable action
____ 11.	CLOISTER	K.	Deeply religious
____ 12.	DESPICABLE	L.	Clever and original
____ 13.	YOKE	M.	Got rid of
____ 14.	OBLIVIOUS	N.	Preservation or deliverance from evil or difficulty
____ 15.	VIGIL	O.	Those who punish lawbreakers themselves instead of relying upon official legal authority
____ 16.	PERPETUALLY	P.	Horrible; deserving only contempt
____ 17.	CONTEMPTIBLE	Q.	Difficult to find, catch, or understand
____ 18.	ELIMINATED	R.	Something to be witnessed because of its impressive nature
____ 19.	MELANCHOLY	S.	With a gentle sadness
____ 20.	FORFEITED	T.	Provoked to anger

The Secret Life of Bees Multiple Choice Unit Test 1 Answer Key

I. Matching

Answer	Term	Description
G	1. LILY	A. Lily yells this, and T. Ray is jolted back to reality.
Q	2. ROSALEEN	B. Lily's place of peace and comfort
T	3. RAY	C. Without her, the colony of bees will die.
P	4. DEBORAH	D. Lily's mother's maiden name
N	5. VIRGINIA	E. Lily's last name
B	6. ORCHARD	F. August's last name
E	7. OWENS	G. She ran away from home.
M	8. TIBURON	H. Lily calls T. Ray from his office.
F	9. BOATWRIGHT	I. Compassionate and sensible bee-keeper
J	10. STREAM	J. Place where Lily and Rosaleen reunite
L	11. LOVE	K. Boatwrights' grandmother: Big ___
R	12. WAILING	L. Bee yard etiquette says you should send the bees this.
O	13. ZACH	M. Written on back of the black Madonna picture: ___ S.C.
H	14. FORREST	N. Home state of Deborah and August
D	15. FONTANEL	O. Lily says he is one-third friend, one-third brother, one-third bee partner, & one-third boyfriend.
A	16. DADDY	P. Lily's mother
K	17. MAMA	Q. Lily helped her escape.
C	18. QUEEN	R. The stone wall is May's ___ wall.
I	19. AUGUST	S. Musician who resents Lily
S	20. JUNE	T. Lily's father; T. ___

II. Multiple Choice

B 1. What does Lily think will give her a "real chance" to learn how to be a beautiful, fashionable girl?

A. A new television show

B. Charm school

C. A fashion magazine subscription

D. A new mother

D 2. What happens when Zach and Lily ride to town to get a new radiator hose?

A. Zach gets Jack Palance's autograph.

B. Zach kisses Lily.

C. Some white men beat up Zach.

D. Zach is arrested.

A 3. What is August's reply when Lily asks if she believes putting black cloths over the hives will help May get to heaven?

A. August says, "Putting black cloths on the hives is for us. I do it to remind us that life gives way into death, and then death turns around and gives way into life."

B. August says, "No, I don't. But I do believe in tradition, that traditions help us get through times like these. So I put on the cloths."

C. August smiles and says, "No, child, I know May has already gone to heaven. The bees know when we're upset, though, and they get upset, too. Covering the hives helps to keep them calmer and happier."

D. August says, "It isn't that the hives are covered, it's the covering of the hives that helps--helps us, not May. Keeping busy distracts us a little and gives us time to accept the loss without being totally focussed on it."

B 4. What important message is in May's note to August and June?

A. "Our Lady of Chains told me this is the best thing for me. I have faith."

B. "It's my time to die, and it's your time to live. Don't mess it up."

C. "I don't want to be a burden to you anymore. The world is too sad of a place for me to be. Be glad I have gone on."

D. "This is nobody's fault. It just is. I no longer need a wailing wall."

A 5. What promise does Zach make to Lily?

A. He says, ". . . one day, after I've gone away and become somebody, I'm gonna find you, and we'll be together then."

B. He says, ". . . and there will come a time when the world will understand that, black or white, we are all human with human hearts and desires. You will always be in my heart, always be my true love, always be my best friend."

C. He says, ". . . just like the honey bee returns home to the hive, I'll come back to you."

D. He says, ". . . and I won't ever let them make you go back to T. Ray."

A 6. Identify Tica Tee.

A. Tica Tee was Lily's mother's imaginary friend.

B. Tica Tee was Lily's mother's favorite doll.

C. Tica Tee was Deborah's nickname for August.

D. Tica Tee is Sugar-Girl's daughter.

A 7. Why do the Daughters of Mary rub honey all over Our Lady?

A. To preserve her

B. To symbolize their sins sticking to her

C. To keep her color black

D. As an offering for the next bee harvest

A 8. Why is the photograph in the hat box so important?

A. The look on her mother's face shows Lily that her mother loved her.

B. It is the only picture of Lily's mother and grandmother together.

C. On the back it says, "My Lovely Lily" in Deborah's own handwriting, a name of endearment proving Lily's mother loved her.

D. It shows Deborah and T. Ray, happy on their wedding day, proving that Deborah and T. Ray really were happy together at least at first.

B 9. What does August tell Lily that she always wants Lily to remember?

A. She says, "Never forget Our Lady."

B. She says, "Our Lady is . . . something *inside* you. "

C. She says, "Our Lady is taking care of your mother--and May--and she is waiting, in time, to take care of you."

D. She says, "You will always have a friend in me--and in Our Lady. She will always give you strength when you are in need, and I shall be here for you as long as I live."

A 10. What is the result of Lily and June's fighting over the water sprinkler?

A. They both end up laughing, and June hugs Lily.

B. Lily gets a bad cut over her left eye, which has to be bandaged.

C. June falls down in the slippery grass, and Lily laughs at her.

D. Lily's face gets covered in mud, and June makes a curt, racial remark.

B 11. What does August say is the whole problem with people?

A. They *think* they are doing good things, but what they choose to do is usually *not* good.

B. They *know* what matters, but they don't *choose* it.

C. People are too blinded by their own prejudices to choose wisely.

D. They are too stupid to see just how prejudiced they are.

B 12. Which is NOT a "scrap of information" Lily knows about her mother?

A. She was an only child.

B. She used to be a waitress.

C. She was from Virginia.

D. She was a lunatic when it came to saving bugs.

C 13. The morning after she is punished for being in the orchard, Lily wakes up late. T. Ray yells at her for not going to work at the peach stand on time. What does Lily understand after T. Ray tells her, "As long as you're under my roof, you'll do what I say!"?

A. She understands why her mother left.

B. She understands that T. Ray is a tyrant.

C. She understands that she needs to leave home.

D. She understands that T. Ray loves her.

A 14. After Lily pours the tear drop out of the bottom of the bee jar, she has a "true religious moment" and hears a voice say something. What does the voice say?

A. It says, "Lily Melissa Owens, your jar is open."

B. It says, "Lily Melissa Owens, that man is holding you back."

C. It says, "Lily Melissa Owens, it's now or never."

D. It says, "Lily Melissa Owens, pray for forgiveness."

D 15. What first lets Lily know she has some prejudice buried inside herself?

A. She is surprised that the sisters keep such a neat, clean house.

B. She is surprised that the sisters speak so well.

C. She is surprised that the food at dinner is just ordinary food.

D. She is surprised that August is so cultured and intelligent.

B 16. For what special help did Lily pray to Mary?

A. ". . . I asked her to make August like me and want to keep me. I asked this daily. . . . "

B. ". . . I asked her to draw a curtain around the pink house so no one would ever find us. I asked this daily. . . . "

C. ". . . I asked her to forgive me. I asked this daily. . . . "

D. ". . . I asked her to help T. Ray learn to be less mean and more forgiving. I asked this daily. . . . "

C 17. Which of these events does NOT happen when Lily goes to touch the heart of Our Lady of Chains?

A. Lily faints.

B. June stops playing music.

C. The Daughters of Mary collectively and spontaneously gasp.

D. Lily freezes with her arm outstretched towards Mary.

D 18. What surprises Zach about Lily?

A. She is younger than he thought.

B. She is older than he thought.

C. She looks so much like her mother.

D. She is white.

D 19. Which of the statements below is NOT something Lily learns from August while they are pasting labels on the jars of honey?

A. She learns how August came to own the house and bee business.

B. She learns how and why the black Madonna came to be on the jar labels.

C. She learns that August lived in Richmond but came here to visit her grandmother.

D. She learns that August was once married, but her husband died.

A 20. What declaration does Lily make to T. Ray?

A. She tells him she will not go back with him.

B. She tells him he has lost.

C. She tells him her mother is dead, and there is nothing either of them can do about that fact.

D. She tells him she will never love him.

IV. Vocabulary

Answer		Word		Definition
R	1.	SPECTACLE	A.	Place of religious seclusion and meditation
F	2.	LURING	B.	Device encircling the necks of a pair of oxen, mules, or other draft animals walking in a team; a restrictive or repressive force
T	3.	RILED	C.	An all-night event spent watching, praying, or guarding
D	4.	BRAZEN	D.	Bold
K	5.	PIOUS	E.	Completely unaware
Q	6.	ELUSIVE	F.	Offering something tempting in order to persuade
N	7.	SALVATION	G.	Undeserving of respect
J	8.	INDIGNATION	H.	Continually; always; without end
O	9.	VIGILANTE	I.	Gave up something willingly
L	10.	INGENIOUS	J.	Anger due to injustice or unreasonable action
A	11.	CLOISTER	K.	Deeply religious
P	12.	DESPICABLE	L.	Clever and original
B	13.	YOKE	M.	Got rid of
E	14.	OBLIVIOUS	N.	Preservation or deliverance from evil or difficulty
C	15.	VIGIL	O.	Those who punish lawbreakers themselves instead of relying upon official legal authority
H	16.	PERPETUALLY	P.	Horrible; deserving only contempt
G	17.	CONTEMPTIBLE	Q.	Difficult to find, catch, or understand
M	18.	ELIMINATED	R.	Something to be witnessed because of its impressive nature
S	19.	MELANCHOLY	S.	With a gentle sadness
I	20.	FORFEITED	T.	Provoked to anger

The Secret Life of Bees Multiple Choice Unit Test 2

I. Matching

____	1.	LILY	A.	Written on back of the black Madonna picture: ___ S.C.
____	2.	ROSALEEN	B.	August covered them with black cloths after May died.
____	3.	RAY	C.	Both of us, it seemed, were doomed to ___.
____	4.	VIRGINIA	D.	The Queen bee is this to every bee in the hive.
____	5.	BUGS	E.	This President signed the Civil Rights Act into law.
____	6.	JOHNSON	F.	Nickname for the Boatwrights: ___ sisters
____	7.	TIBURON	G.	Deborah was a lunatic when it came to saving these.
____	8.	STEW	H.	She ran away from home.
____	9.	PINK	I.	The most important item in the hat box
____	10.	MAY	J.	Compassionate and sensible bee-keeper
____	11.	NEIL	K.	Lily says he is one-third friend, one-third brother, one-third bee partner, & one-third boyfriend.
____	12.	ZACH	L.	He wants to marry June.
____	13.	MOTHER	M.	___ don't help anything. You know that.
____	14.	HIVES	N.	Color of the Boatwrights' house
____	15.	CALENDAR	O.	Lily's father; T. ___
____	16.	PICTURE	P.	Home state of Deborah and August
____	17.	MISERY	Q.	She lacks built-in protection around her heart.
____	18.	REGRETS	R.	Lily helped her escape.
____	19.	BLUE	S.	Lily's favorite color
____	20.	AUGUST	T.	Frogmore ___ General Store

II. Multiple Choice

1. Lily wakes up T. Ray in the middle of the night to show him something. What does she want to show him?
   A. Lily wants to show T. Ray the swarm of bees in her room.
   B. Lily wants to show T. Ray a poem she wrote.
   C. Lily wants to show T. Ray that a bee has stung her.
   D. Lily wants to show T. Ray some things she found in the attic.

2. What important message is in May's note to August and June?
   A. "I don't want to be a burden to you anymore. The world is too sad of a place for me to be. Be glad I have gone on."
   B. "Our Lady of Chains told me this is the best thing for me. I have faith."
   C. "This is nobody's fault. It just is. I no longer need a wailing wall."
   D. "It's my time to die, and it's your time to live. Don't mess it up."

3. Which is NOT a reason Lily leaves the honey house while everyone seems to be meditating with Our Lady of Chains?
   A. She can't stand to see Mary wrapped in chains.
   B. She doesn't want to remember the past.
   C. She doesn't want to meditate.
   D. She feels like she is about to faint and needs fresh air.

4. What promise does Zach make to Lily?
   A. He says, ". . . just like the honey bee returns home to the hive, I'll come back to you."
   B. He says, ". . . one day, after I've gone away and become somebody, I'm gonna find you, and we'll be together then."
   C. He says, ". . . and I won't ever let them make you go back to T. Ray."
   D. He says, ". . . and there will come a time when the world will understand that, black or white, we are all human with human hearts and desires. You will always be in my heart, always be my true love, always be my best friend."

5. What does August tell Lily about her mother that makes Lily say, "I hate her"?
   A. August tells Lily that Deborah came to Tiburon by herself; she had left Lily with T. Ray.
   B. August tells Lily that Deborah had gone to charm school and graduated at the top of her class.
   C. August tells Lily that Deborah was a beautiful little girl with everything a little girl could want.
   D. August tells Lily that Deborah had tried to commit suicide when she found out that she was pregnant.

6. What are August's parting words to Lily as she stands in the doorway after putting her to bed on the night of their big conversation?
   A. She says, "There is nothing perfect. There is only life."
   B. She says, "Your mother certainly forgives you, but you will never be happy until you forgive yourself."
   C. She says, "If T. Ray comes, we'll have no choice."
   D. She says, "Sleep well, Daughter of Mary."

7. How does having her mother's things and knowing the whole story affect Lily? What does she do?
   A. Lily pulls away into herself, wanting to be alone.
   B. Lily has never been happier. She asks August if they can have a Deborah Day to celebrate her mother's life.
   C. Lily's mind is finally at rest; she is happy and carefree at last.
   D. Lily feels the need to confront T. Ray, and she asks August if she would drive her to see him.

8. Which of the following did NOT happen when T. Ray found out that Deborah had been at the Boatwrights' when she left him?
   A. T. Ray lost himself for a bit and confused Lily with Deborah.
   B. T. Ray threatened Lily with a knife.
   C. T. Ray hit Lily and told her she would never leave him again.
   D. T. Ray made Lily kneel down on grits.

9. What does August do to help diffuse the situation between T. Ray and Lily?
   A. She invites T. Ray to stay to dinner, to talk about things and to calmly straighten things out. She warmly welcomes him into her home and is clearly willing to share Lily with him.
   B. She starts talking to T. Ray about Deborah and the early, happier days of their marriage.
   C. She gives him a way out of the situation by saying he would be doing them a favor to let Lily stay.
   D. She brings out the hat box with Deborah's things in it and offers it to T. Ray.

10. What sets off May just before she insists on going to the wall by herself?
   A. She learns that Dr. Martin Luther King, Jr. has been killed.
   B. Rosaleen tells May the truth about herself and Lily.
   C. She learns that Lily is Deborah's daughter.
   D. She learns that Zach has been arrested.

11. What is the result of Lily and June's fighting over the water sprinkler?
   A. They both end up laughing, and June hugs Lily.
   B. June falls down in the slippery grass, and Lily laughs at her.
   C. Lily gets a bad cut over her left eye, which has to be bandaged.
   D. Lily's face gets covered in mud, and June makes a curt, racial remark.

12. Why does T. Ray make Lily kneel down on the Martha White grits?
   A. He thinks she has become too sassy.
   B. He thinks she has been in the orchard with a boy.
   C. He thinks she needs to learn self-discipline.
   D. He thinks capturing the bees is cruel.

13. Which of the following is NOT something for which Rosaleen is arrested?
   A. Theft
   B. Disturbing the Peace
   C. Assault
   D. Grand Larceny

14. After Lily and Rosaleen are dropped off outside of Tiburon, they have a fight and part ways for a short while. Where do they get back together?

   A. In a stream
   B. Alongside the road
   C. In a boat
   D. In the woods

15. What does May do when an unpleasant topic is brought up?

   A. May begins laughing hysterically.
   B. May starts frantically singing, "Oh! Susanna."
   C. May changes the topic immediately.
   D. May runs from the room.

16. Which is NOT one of the rules for "bee yard etiquette"?

   A. Don't swat.
   B. Don't shake the smoker.
   C. Send the bees love.
   D. Don't be afraid.

17. Who are The Daughters of Mary?

   A. They are a group of friends who get together every week just to chat and have fun.
   B. They are a group of black women devoted to Civil Rights and Women's Rights.
   C. They are Queenie, Sugar, Neil, and the Boatwright sisters.
   D. They are a group of women (and one man) who meet at the Boatwrights' house to honor and pray to Mary, the mother of Jesus.

18. Lily tells Zach, "You've got to hear of these things before you can imagine them." What is Zach's response?

   A. He says, "Imagination is God's greatest gift to man."
   B. He says, "Hearing things isn't everything."
   C. He says, "Not me."
   D. He says, "You've gotta imagine what's never been."

19. How does Lily feel when she and August go to collect honey, and the bees come out and fly around her?

    A. She feels like she is the center of all their comforting.
    B. She feels like she is the object of their attack.
    C. The bees remind her of a posse, and she thinks about T. Ray and the police coming after her.
    D. She feels like she is part of the swarm . . . a bee, carefree and secure for the first time in her life.

20. Lily runs after T. Ray as he leaves, yelling for him to stop. What does she ask him, and what is his response?

    A. Lily asks him if he loves her at all. He tells her he does not.
    B. Lily asks him if she can come visit him sometimes. He says, "Yes."
    C. Lily asks him what her favorite color is. He says, "Blue."
    D. Lily asks him if she really did kill her mother. He tells her she did.

III. Composition

1. What does Our Lady of Chains become to Lily?

2. The issue of "mother" and motherhood is a big part of the book. What mothers and mother figures are present in the book? What points does the author make about mothers and motherhood? Explain.

3. There are many references to praying and religion in the book. What points does the author make about religion through the events in the book? Explain fully.

4. August seems to be a very special person. What are her best qualities? Does she have any negative traits? If so, what are they?

IV. Vocabulary

____	1.	PRESUMPTUOUS	A.	Expression of grief
____	2.	ORNERINESS	B.	Tiny
____	3.	COAX	C.	Lessen or become distant
____	4.	ELUSIVE	D.	Excessively forward or confident
____	5.	AGITATES	E.	Hard-working
____	6.	IMMUNITY	F.	Able; competent
____	7.	RECEDE	G.	Lazy
____	8.	DRONES	H.	Consider; think deeply about
____	9.	INNATE	I.	Male bees that mate with the queen
____	10.	MINISCULE	J.	Difficult to find, catch, or understand
____	11.	GEYSER	K.	Spring that regularly, forcefully ejects a stream of hot water or steam up into the air
____	12.	SHIFTLESS	L.	Stubborn and irritable attitude
____	13.	CREVICE	M.	Stirs up
____	14.	CONCOCT	N.	Someone who cannot remember
____	15.	INDUSTRIOUS	O.	Gently persuade
____	16.	MULL	P.	Invent; make up
____	17.	AMNESIAC	Q.	Large number or variety
____	18.	ARRAY	R.	Exemption or protection from danger
____	19.	CAPABLE	S.	Narrow crack
____	20.	LAMENT	T.	Possessed at birth; inborn

The Secret Life of Bees Multiple Choice Unit Test 2 Answer Key

I. Matching

H	1. LILY	A. Written on back of the black Madonna picture: ___ S.C.
R	2. ROSALEEN	B. August covered them with black cloths after May died.
O	3. RAY	C. Both of us, it seemed, were doomed to ___.
P	4. VIRGINIA	D. The Queen bee is this to every bee in the hive.
G	5. BUGS	E. This President signed the Civil Rights Act into law.
E	6. JOHNSON	F. Nickname for the Boatwrights: ___ sisters
A	7. TIBURON	G. Deborah was a lunatic when it came to saving these.
T	8. STEW	H. She ran away from home.
N	9. PINK	I. The most important item in the hat box
Q	10. MAY	J. Compassionate and sensible bee-keeper
L	11. NEIL	K. Lily says he is one-third friend, one-third brother, one-third bee partner, & one-third boyfriend.
K	12. ZACH	L. He wants to marry June.
D	13. MOTHER	M. ___ don't help anything. You know that.
B	14. HIVES	N. Color of the Boatwrights' house
F	15. CALENDAR	O. Lily's father; T. ___
I	16. PICTURE	P. Home state of Deborah and August
C	17. MISERY	Q. She lacks built-in protection around her heart.
M	18. REGRETS	R. Lily helped her escape.
S	19. BLUE	S. Lily's favorite color
J	20. AUGUST	T. Frogmore ___ General Store

II. Multiple Choice

A 1. Lily wakes up T. Ray in the middle of the night to show him something. What does she want to show him?

A. Lily wants to show T. Ray the swarm of bees in her room.
B. Lily wants to show T. Ray a poem she wrote.
C. Lily wants to show T. Ray that a bee has stung her.
D. Lily wants to show T. Ray some things she found in the attic.

D 2. What important message is in May's note to August and June?

A. "I don't want to be a burden to you anymore. The world is too sad of a place for me to be. Be glad I have gone on."
B. "Our Lady of Chains told me this is the best thing for me. I have faith."
C. "This is nobody's fault. It just is. I no longer need a wailing wall."
D. "It's my time to die, and it's your time to live. Don't mess it up."

D 3. Which is NOT a reason Lily leaves the honey house while everyone seems to be meditating with Our Lady of Chains?

A. She can't stand to see Mary wrapped in chains.
B. She doesn't want to remember the past.
C. She doesn't want to meditate.
D. She feels like she is about to faint and needs fresh air.

B 4. What promise does Zach make to Lily?

A. He says, ". . . just like the honey bee returns home to the hive, I'll come back to you."
B. He says, ". . . one day, after I've gone away and become somebody, I'm gonna find you, and we'll be together then."
C. He says, ". . . and I won't ever let them make you go back to T. Ray."
D. He says, ". . . and there will come a time when the world will understand that, black or white, we are all human with human hearts and desires. You will always be in my heart, always be my true love, always be my best friend."

A 5. What does August tell Lily about her mother that makes Lily say, "I hate her"?

A. August tells Lily that Deborah came to Tiburon by herself; she had left Lily with T. Ray.

B. August tells Lily that Deborah had gone to charm school and graduated at the top of her class.

C. August tells Lily that Deborah was a beautiful little girl with everything a little girl could want.

D. August tells Lily that Deborah had tried to commit suicide when she found out that she was pregnant.

A 6. What are August's parting words to Lily as she stands in the doorway after putting her to bed on the night of their big conversation?

A. She says, "There is nothing perfect. There is only life."

B. She says, "Your mother certainly forgives you, but you will never be happy until you forgive yourself."

C. She says, "If T. Ray comes, we'll have no choice."

D. She says, "Sleep well, Daughter of Mary."

A 7. How does having her mother's things and knowing the whole story affect Lily? What does she do?

A. Lily pulls away into herself, wanting to be alone.

B. Lily has never been happier. She asks August if they can have a Deborah Day to celebrate her mother's life.

C. Lily's mind is finally at rest; she is happy and carefree at last.

D. Lily feels the need to confront T. Ray, and she asks August if she would drive her to see him.

D 8. Which of the following did NOT happen when T. Ray found out that Deborah had been at the Boatwrights' when she left him?

A. T. Ray lost himself for a bit and confused Lily with Deborah.

B. T. Ray threatened Lily with a knife.

C. T. Ray hit Lily and told her she would never leave him again.

D. T. Ray made Lily kneel down on grits.

C 9. What does August do to help diffuse the situation between T. Ray and Lily?

A. She invites T. Ray to stay to dinner, to talk about things and to calmly straighten things out. She warmly welcomes him into her home and is clearly willing to share Lily with him.

B. She starts talking to T. Ray about Deborah and the early, happier days of their marriage.

C. She gives him a way out of the situation by saying he would be doing them a favor to let Lily stay.

D. She brings out the hat box with Deborah's things in it and offers it to T. Ray.

D 10. What sets off May just before she insists on going to the wall by herself?

A. She learns that Dr. Martin Luther King, Jr. has been killed.

B. Rosaleen tells May the truth about herself and Lily.

C. She learns that Lily is Deborah's daughter.

D. She learns that Zach has been arrested.

A 11. What is the result of Lily and June's fighting over the water sprinkler?

A. They both end up laughing, and June hugs Lily.

B. June falls down in the slippery grass, and Lily laughs at her.

C. Lily gets a bad cut over her left eye, which has to be bandaged.

D. Lily's face gets covered in mud, and June makes a curt, racial remark.

B 12. Why does T. Ray make Lily kneel down on the Martha White grits?

A. He thinks she has become too sassy.

B. He thinks she has been in the orchard with a boy.

C. He thinks she needs to learn self-discipline.

D. He thinks capturing the bees is cruel.

D 13. Which of the following is NOT something for which Rosaleen is arrested?

A. Theft

B. Disturbing the Peace

C. Assault

D. Grand Larceny

A 14. After Lily and Rosaleen are dropped off outside of Tiburon, they have a fight and part ways for a short while. Where do they get back together?

A. In a stream
B. Alongside the road
C. In a boat
D. In the woods

B 15. What does May do when an unpleasant topic is brought up?

A. May begins laughing hysterically.
B. May starts frantically singing, "Oh! Susanna."
C. May changes the topic immediately.
D. May runs from the room.

B 16. Which is NOT one of the rules for "bee yard etiquette"?

A. Don't swat.
B. Don't shake the smoker.
C. Send the bees love.
D. Don't be afraid.

D 17. Who are The Daughters of Mary?

A. They are a group of friends who get together every week just to chat and have fun.
B. They are a group of black women devoted to Civil Rights and Women's Rights.
C. They are Queenie, Sugar, Neil, and the Boatwright sisters.
D. They are a group of women (and one man) who meet at the Boatwrights' house to honor and pray to Mary, the mother of Jesus.

D 18. Lily tells Zach, "You've got to hear of these things before you can imagine them." What is Zach's response?

A. He says, "Imagination is God's greatest gift to man."
B. He says, "Hearing things isn't everything."
C. He says, "Not me."
D. He says, "You've gotta imagine what's never been."

A 19. How does Lily feel when she and August go to collect honey, and the bees come out and fly around her?

A. She feels like she is the center of all their comforting.

B. She feels like she is the object of their attack.

C. The bees remind her of a posse, and she thinks about T. Ray and the police coming after her.

D. She feels like she is part of the swarm . . . a bee, carefree and secure for the first time in her life.

D 20. Lily runs after T. Ray as he leaves, yelling for him to stop. What does she ask him, and what is his response?

A. Lily asks him if he loves her at all. He tells her he does not.

B. Lily asks him if she can come visit him sometimes. He says, "Yes."

C. Lily asks him what her favorite color is. He says, "Blue."

D. Lily asks him if she really did kill her mother. He tells her she did.

IV. Vocabulary

D	1. PRESUMPTUOUS	A. Expression of grief
L	2. ORNERINESS	B. Tiny
O	3. COAX	C. Lessen or become distant
J	4. ELUSIVE	D. Excessively forward or confident
M	5. AGITATES	E. Hard-working
R	6. IMMUNITY	F. Able; competent
C	7. RECEDE	G. Lazy
I	8. DRONES	H. Consider; think deeply about
T	9. INNATE	I. Male bees that mate with the queen
B	10. MINISCULE	J. Difficult to find, catch, or understand
K	11. GEYSER	K. Spring that regularly, forcefully ejects a stream of hot water or steam up into the air
G	12. SHIFTLESS	L. Stubborn and irritable attitude
S	13. CREVICE	M. Stirs up
P	14. CONCOCT	N. Someone who cannot remember
E	15. INDUSTRIOUS	O. Gently persuade
H	16. MULL	P. Invent; make up
N	17. AMNESIAC	Q. Large number or variety
Q	18. ARRAY	R. Exemption or protection from danger
F	19. CAPABLE	S. Narrow crack
A	20. LAMENT	T. Possessed at birth; inborn

UNIT RESOURCE MATERIALS

BULLETIN BOARD IDEAS *The Secret Life of Bees*

1. Save one corner of the board for the best of students' *Secret Life of Bees* writing assignments.
2. Take one of the word search puzzles from the resource materials section and, with a marker, copy it over in a large size on the bulletin board. Write the clue words to find to one side. Invite students prior to and after class to find the words and circle them on the bulletin board.
3. Write several of the most significant quotes from the book onto the board on brightly colored paper.
4. Make a bulletin board listing the vocabulary words for this unit. As you complete sections of the novel and discuss the vocabulary for each section, write the definitions on the bulletin board. (If your board is one students face frequently, it will help them learn the words.)
5. Have students bring in photographs of themselves with their parents or grandparents (or any "mothers" in their lives). They may also bring in samples of hobbies/skills or pictures relating to hobbies/skills that they learned from these individuals.
6. Track an on-going news item regarding an issue that is important to teenagers, sutdents, or society as a whole. Post articles from various newspapers as the story progresses. Students may bring in articles, as well. Discuss the point of view of each article, any signs of "slanted" reporting, and how the "slant" is achieved through words.
7. Have students write news articles for the main events of the story as the story progresses and post them on the board with headlines. Point out any different points of view or different slants to the news stories written.
8. Post examples of allusions from the list of allusions in the daily lessons--and any photos or pictures you can find related to those things.
9. Post a map of the South pinpointing where important events relating to the civil rights movement happened, and running a string to an article about each.
10. Make a bulletin board about the various issues addressed in the book and ways to cope with those kinds of issues, including hotline numbers and help contact information.
11. Make a bulletin board about BEES! Invite students to bring in pictures of different kinds of bees and short articles, poems, or quips/quotes about bees to post on the board.
12. Make a bulletin board about HONEY--how it is made, uses, folklore, etc. Invite students to bring in articles, pictures, recipies, etc. to post.
13. There are many images of black Madonnas available on the Internet. Invite students to do a search for pictures of black Madonnas and bring them in to post. Articles about the history or more information about their Madonnas would be good to post next to the pictures.
14. Make a bulletin board about the 1960s. Invite students to bring in pictures, items that can be attached to the bulletin board, quotes, poems, music lyrics, etc.--anything that is related to the 1960's. Find a pair of fishnet stockings, a tie-dyed t-shirt, a photocopy of an old album cover, a 45 single record, a peace symbol, a picture of a volkswagon bug or a hippie bus, something with "flower power," etc.
15. Get 2 copies of *The Three Little Pigs* and 2 copies of *The True Story of the Three Little Pigs*. Take the books apart, and post the pages in order on the bulletin board (like a cartoon strip), each telling the story of The Three Little Pigs from a different point of view.

RELATED TOPICS *The Secret Life of Bees*

1. Uncle Wiggly
2. Segregation
3. Bees
4. Honey
5. Roaches
6. Keeping Vigil
7. Peaches
8. Ralph Waldo Emerson
9. Queen For A Day
10. Eleanor Roosevelt
11. Catholics, Baptists, & Methodists
12. Walden Pond
13. Wimbledon (Tennis)
14. Gun Safety
15. History of Television
16. Fort Sumter
17. Blue Laws
18. Fats Domino
19. Nat King Cole
20. Kamikaze Planes
21. Niagra Falls (people in barrels going over)
22. Moses Taking People Out Of Egypt
23. Shakespeare
24. Wailing Wall
25. Wilt Chamberlain
26. Walter Cronkite
27. Cars & Trucks of the Early 1960's
28. Saigon
29. Malcolm X
30. Sunbeam Bread
31. Jim Crow
32. *Go Tell It On The Mountain*
33. President Johnson
34. The Civil Rights Act
35. *The $64,000 Question*
36. Emily Dickinson
37. Jack Palance
38. *The Fugitive*
39. Honeycomb
40. Gabriel and Mary

41. Our Lady of the Chains
42. Shirley Temple
43. Martha White
44. Soda Fountain
45. Fidel Castro
46. Goldwater For President
47. Hula Hoops
48. African-American Voter Registration
49. Charm Bracelets
50. The Madonna
51. *Oh, Susanna!*
52. *Stopping By The Woods On A Snowy Evening*
53. Martin Luther King, Jr.
54. Sophia Loren
55. Kruschev
56. The Beatles

MORE ACTIVITIES *The Secret Life of Bees*

1. Have students work together to make a time line of the events in the story. Take a large piece of construction paper and on one wall (or however you can physically arrange it in your room) make the events of the story along it. In addition to a written description, students may want to add drawings or cut-out pictures to represent the events.
2. Have students design a book cover (front/back/inside flaps) for *The Secret Life of Bees*.
3. Have students design a bulletin board (ready to put up, not just sketched) for *The Secret Life of Bees*.
4. Share *A Wreath for Emmett Till* by Marilyn Nelson with your students, including the background information. Discuss their reactions to the work. This may stretch into a more in-depth analysis of the Nelson work, which is a unique sonnet rich with allusion, emotion, and literary beauty. This could also serve as a transition to the next unit: poetry, historical fiction, Civil Rights, African-American literature, etc. (*A Wreath for Emmett Till* is available at www.tpet.com under the title *Secret Life of Bees*)
5. Have students share their childhood experiences in a variety of ways: they may put together a class anthology that collects their childhood memories of visits to family members' houses; they may describe the first time they learned to do something; they may recall parents' friends or family members--really anything related to childhood memories. Each student could create one page with a drawing and a paragraph or poem about his/her favorite childhood memory (or a memory of a "mother" in his/her life) for a class booklet.
6. On page 271 of *The Secret Life of Bees*, Lily "spent twenty minutes on this fascinating question: if you could have one miracle from the Bible happen to you, what would it be?" Use this as an in-class activity. Brainstorm "miracles" from the Bible. Let students each pick one and write about why they would choose that miracle to happen to them.
7. Have students or groups of students make different recipies containing honey. Bring them all in on one day (or each person/group could bring one thing on different days throughout the unit) for everyone to taste. Publish a recipie book at the end.
8. Create a "wailing wall" for your classroom using garden border stones or something as simple as a class set of dictionaries stacked with spaces between. Invite students to put scraps of paper with a word or two identifying their troubles in the cracks.
9. Visit a peach (or other kind of) orchard if you have one close by. Learn about the orchard industry and how it works.
10. Invite a guest speaker in for a day to talk to your students about one of these topics:

    Coping With Things Life Throws At You; Loss and Grieving; Suicide Feeling; Abandoned/Unwanted

    Making Good Choices

    The Civil Rights Struggle (historic); Personal Rememberances Before the Civil Rights Act; Overcoming Prejudice

    Catholicism; The Virgin Mary's Place in Religion; The Rosary; Praying

    Motherhood; Being a Parent

    The 1960s

    Beekeeping

QUOTATIONS *The Secret Life of Bees*

1. "You ain't touching that chick." (11)

2. It was a secret knowledge that would slip up and overwhelm me, and I would take off running--even if it was raining out, I ran--straight down the hill to my special place in the peach orchard. I'd lie right down on the ground and it would calm me. (17)

3. "Would it be too much to ask you to get out to the peach stand and do some work? You're not Queen for a Day, you know." (25)

4. "As long as you're under my roof, you'll do what I say!" (26)

5. Every time a rumor got going about a group of Negroes coming to worship with us on Sunday morning, the deacons stood locked-arms across the church steps to turn them away. We loved them in the Lord, Brother Gerald said, but they had their own places. (30)

6. I had gone once in a raft down the Chattooga River with my church group, and the same feeling came to me now--of being lifted by the currents, by a swirl of events I couldn't reverse. (32)

7. "I can't say what men riled up like that will do." (35)

8. "The day she died, she'd come back to get her things, that's all. You can hate me all you want, but she's the one who left you." (39)

9. But I had such a moment right then, standing in my own ordinary room. I heard a voice say, *Lily Melissa Owens, your jar is open.* (41)

10. "Oh, Lily, what have we gone and done?" (65)

11. If only she could get some manners. (75)

12. "But she's white, August." (87)

13. "They called her Our Lady of Chains because she broke them." (110)

14. She stopped right in the middle of the song, and I was left in the silence with my hand stretched out. (111)

15. "You've gotta imagine what's never been." (121)

16. "Or maybe desire kicked in when it pleased without noticing the rules we lived and died by." (126)

17. "I loved him enough--I just loved my freedom more." (146)

18. "I was gonna say, The trouble is they [people] know what matters, but they don't choose it." (147)

19. I loved the idea of bees having a secret life, just like the one I was living. (148)

20. "--they know the queen is their mother. She is the mother of thousands." (149)

21. It felt like the queen's attendants were out here in a frenzy of love, caressing me in a thousand places. *Look who's here, it's Lily. She is so weary and lost. Come on, bee sisters.* I was the stamen in the middle of a twirling flower. The center of all their comforting. (151)

22. "Actually, you can be bad at something, Lily, but if you love doing it, that will be enough." (167)

23. June Boatwright hugged me while our clothes made sweet, squish sounds up and down our bodies. (170)

24. "Oh, yes. Deborah Fontanel. She stayed out there in the honey house. She was the sweetest thing." (173)

25. Rosaleen reminded me of the stature of Our Lady in the parlor, and I thought, *If August is the red heart on Mary's chest, Rosaleen is the fist*. (182)

26. May walking into the trees with the little circle of light bobbing in front of her, then swallowed up by the dark. (188)

27. Here's the translation: *I am completely confused what a white girl like you is doing staying in a colored house*. (197)

28. They didn't even think of me being different. (209)

29. It's my time to die, and it's your time to live. Don't mess it up. (210)

30. "You are one-third friend, one-third brother, one-third bee partner, and one-third boyfriend." (216)

31. . . . I could see the struggle in her face. The surrender she had to make inside. Not just to Neil but to life. Finally she let out a long, sighing breath. "All right," she said, "Let's get married." (222)

32. "It is only a reenactment," August had said. "To help us remember. Remembering is everything." Still, the whole idea wrapped me in sadness. I hated remembering. (228)

33. ". . . one day, after I've gone away and become somebody, I'm gonna find you, and we'll be together then." (231)

34. "There's a fullness of time for things, Lily. You have to know when to prod and when to be quiet, when to let things take their course." (236)

35. *You are unlovable, Lily Owens. Unlovable. Who could love you? Who in this world could ever love you?* (242)

36. "You know, Lily, people can start out one way, and by the time life gets through with them they end up completely different." (248)

37. Knowing can be a curse on a person's life. I'd traded a pack of lies for a pack of truth, and I didn't know which one was heavier. (255)

38. There is nothing perfect. . . . There is only life. (256)

39. "Oh, Lily. Why would I go and hurt you with something like that?" (265)

40. If God said in plain language, "I'm giving you a choice, forgive or die," a lot of people would go ahead and order their coffin. (277)

41. "Regrets don't help anything, you know that." (280)

42. I wanted to say, *Rosaleen, you know what? I'm proud of you.* (282)

43. Both of us, it seemed like, were doomed to misery. (283)

44. "Our Lady is not some magical being out there somewhere, like a fairy godmother. She's not the statue in the parlor. She's something inside of you. Do you understand what I'm telling you?" (288)

45. I remember the sight of them standing there waiting. All these women, all this love, waiting. (299)

46. I have more mothers than any eight girls off the street. They are the moons shining over me. (302)

UNIT WORD LIST *The Secret Life of Bees*

No.	Word	Clue/Definition
1.	ANGRY	Why Lily wrecked the honey house
2.	APRIL	She committed suicide at age 15.
3.	AUGUST	Compassionate and sensible bee-keeper
4.	BECCA	Clayton Forrest's daughter
5.	BEES	The Secret Life of ___
6.	BLUE	Lily's favorite color
7.	BOATWRIGHT	August's last name
8.	BRACELET	Birthday present Lily wants: charm ___
9.	BUGS	Deborah was a lunatic when it came to saving these.
10.	CALENDAR	Nickname for the Boatwrights: ___ sisters
11.	CHAINS	Our Lady of ___
12.	CHARM	Lily thinks this school will give her a real chance to be beautiful and fashionable.
13.	CHICK	You ain't touchin' that ___.
14.	DADDY	Lily yells this, and T. Ray is jolted back to reality.
15.	DEBORAH	Lily's mother
16.	DROWNS	How May dies
17.	FAINTS	Lily does this the first time she tries to touch Our Lady's heart.
18.	FAN	Item Rosaleen steals from the church
19.	FONTANEL	Lily's mother's maiden name
20.	FORREST	Lily calls T. Ray from his office.
21.	FOUR	Lily's age when she accidentally shot her mother
22.	GABRIEL	In every picture, he had a big white lily for Mary.
23.	GASTON	He tells Lily to hush when Rosaleen is struck with the flashlight.
24.	GRITS	T. Ray makes Lily kneel on these.
25.	HENRY	Mrs. ___ helps Lily realize she is smart.
26.	HIVES	August covered them with black cloths after May died.
27.	HONEY	Little building where Lily stayed: the ___ house
28.	IMPULSIVE	Trait common to Lily and Deborah
29.	JAR	Home for the bees Lily catches
30.	JOHNSON	This President signed the Civil Rights Act into law.
31.	JUNE	Musician who resents Lily
32.	KIDD	Author
33.	LAW	Zach wants a career in this field.
34.	LILY	She ran away from home.
35.	LOVE	Bee yard etiquette says you should send the bees this.
36.	MADONNA	The black ___ picture led Lily to August.
37.	MAMA	Boatwrights' grandmother: Big ___
38.	MARY	Daughters of ___

No.	Word	Clue/Definition
39.	MAY	She lacks built-in protection around her heart.
40.	MISERY	Both of us, it seemed, were doomed to ___.
41.	MOTHER	The Queen bee is this to every bee in the hive.
42.	NEIL	He wants to marry June.
43.	NOTE	May left one for August and June.
44.	NOTEBOOK	Zach's gift to Lily
45.	OPEN	Lily Melissa Owens, your jar is ___.
46.	ORCHARD	Lily's place of peace and comfort
47.	OWENS	Lily's last name
48.	PAPER	Scraps of this are stuck into the stone wall.
49.	PEACH	Place where Lily worked: ___ stand
50.	PEANUTS	August and Lily like this in their Coke.
51.	PICTURE	The most important item in the hat box
52.	PIN	Object Lily wears that holds T. Ray's attention
53.	PINK	Color of the Boatwrights' house
54.	QUEEN	Without her, the colony of bees will die.
55.	RACE	It is a major issue in the novel.
56.	RAY	Lily's father; T. ___
57.	REGRETS	___ don't help anything. You know that.
58.	ROACHES	May and Deborah lured these out of the house with graham cracker & marshmallow crumbs.
59.	ROSALEEN	Lily helped her escape.
60.	SPRINKLER	June and Lily wrestle over it.
61.	STEW	Frogmore ___ General Store
62.	STREAM	Place where Lily and Rosaleen reunite
63.	SUSANNA	May's song: O! ___
64.	TIBURON	Written on back of the black Madonna picture: ___ S.C.
65.	TICA	Deborah's imaginary friend: ___ Tee
66.	TOMATOES	June throws these at Neil.
67.	VIRGINIA	Home state of Deborah and August
68.	VOTE	Rosaleen wants to register to do this.
69.	WAILING	The stone wall is May's ___ wall.
70.	WHISTLE	Bee yard etiquette says if you are angry you should do this.
71.	ZACH	Lily says he is one-third friend, one-third brother, one-third bee partner, & one-third boyfriend.

CROSSWORD - The Secret Life of Bees

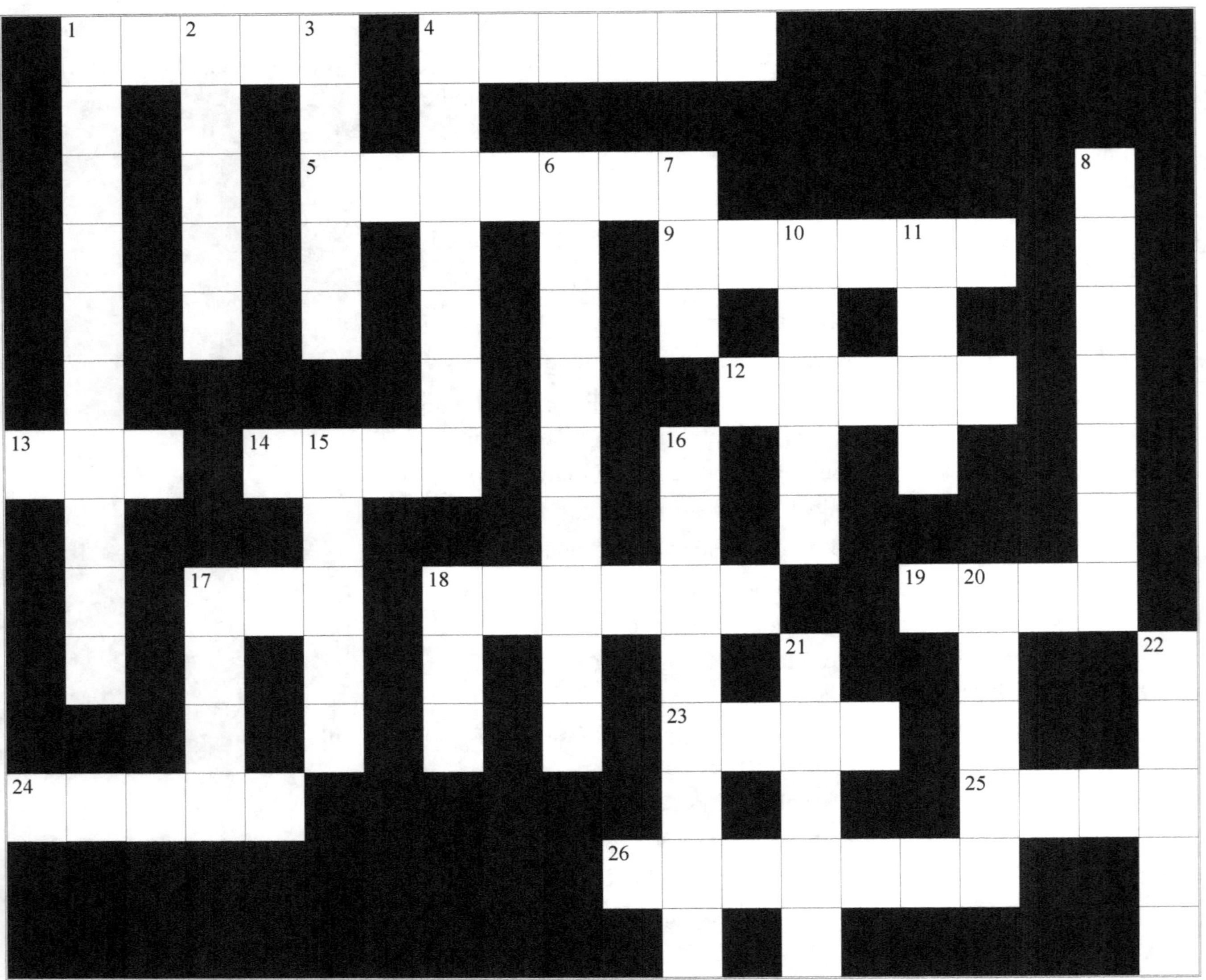

Across
1. Clayton Forrest's daughter
4. How May dies
5. In every picture he had a white lily for Mary.
9. Compassionate and sensible beekeeper
12. August covered them with black cloths.
13. Object Lily wears that holds T. Ray's attention
14. One-third each friend, brother, bee partner & boyfriend to Lily
17. Home for the bees Lily catches
18. Lily ____ when she first tries to touch Our Lady's heart.
19. Rosaleen wants to register to do this.
23. The Secret Life of ___
24. Where Lily stayed: ____ house
25. May left one for August and June.
26. May & Deborah lured them out with crumbs.

Down
1. August's last name
2. You ain't touchin' that ____.
3. Why Lily wrecked the honey house
4. Lily's mother
6. Trait common to Lily and Deborah
7. Zach wants a career in this field.
8. Most important item in the hat box
10. T. Ray makes Lily kneel on these.
11. Frogmore ___ General Store
15. She committed suicide at age 15.
16. Zach's gift to Lily
17. Musician who resents Lily
18. Item Rosaleen steals from church
20. Lily's last name
21. Place where Lily worked: ___ stand
22. Without her, the colony of bees will die.

ANSWER KEY CROSSWORD - The Secret Life of Bees

	1 B	E	2 C	C	3 A		4 D	R	O	W	N	S							
	O		H		N		E												
	A		I		5 G	A	B	R	6 I	E	7 L							8 P	
	T		C		R		O		M		9 A	U	10 G	U	11 S	T		I	
	W		K		Y		R		P		W		R		T			C	
	R						A		U			12 H	I	V	E	S		T	
13 P	I	N		14 Z	15 A	C	H		L		16 N		T		W			U	
	G				P				S		O		S					R	
	H		17 J	A	R		18 F	A	I	N	T	S			19 V	20 O	T	E	
	T		U		I		A		V		E		21 P			W			22 Q
			N		L		N		E		23 B	E	E	S		E			U
24 H	O	N	E	Y							O		A			25 N	O	T	E
										26 R	O	A	C	H	E	S			E
											K		H						N

Across
1. Clayton Forrest's daughter
4. How May dies
5. In every picture he had a white lily for Mary.
9. Compassionate and sensible beekeeper
12. August covered them with black cloths.
13. Object Lily wears that holds T. Ray's attention
14. One-third each friend, brother, bee partner & boyfriend to Lily
17. Home for the bees Lily catches
18. Lily ____ when she first tries to touch Our Lady's heart.
19. Rosaleen wants to register to do this.
23. The Secret Life of ___
24. Where Lily stayed: ____ house
25. May left one for August and June.
26. May & Deborah lured them out with crumbs.

Down
1. August's last name
2. You ain't touchin' that ____.
3. Why Lily wrecked the honey house
4. Lily's mother
6. Trait common to Lily and Deborah
7. Zach wants a career in this field.
8. Most important item in the hat box
10. T. Ray makes Lily kneel on these.
11. Frogmore ___ General Store
15. She committed suicide at age 15.
16. Zach's gift to Lily
17. Musician who resents Lily
18. Item Rosaleen steals from church
20. Lily's last name
21. Place where Lily worked: ___ stand
22. Without her, the colony of bees will die.

WORD SEARCH - The Secret Life of Bees

B	R	A	C	E	L	E	T	R	C	T	P	K	M	A	Y	G	L	R	Z
E	G	P	H	G	E	B	E	E	T	H	R	I	I	H	Q	A	O	A	D
E	A	F	A	N	N	P	W	L	O	G	I	O	N	D	X	S	V	Y	Y
S	B	Y	R	B	A	B	A	K	M	I	V	C	S	K	D	T	E	R	R
I	R	R	M	P	T	E	I	N	A	R	V	T	K	A	W	O	G	N	L
M	I	E	R	F	N	C	L	I	T	W	C	O	I	E	L	N	E	E	R
P	E	S	G	O	O	C	I	R	O	T	W	D	T	B	A	E	P	P	R
U	L	I	D	R	F	A	N	P	E	A	Z	S	Q	E	U	B	E	O	T
L	Z	M	S	R	E	D	G	S	S	O	D	A	W	Q	A	R	U	N	F
S	M	D	G	E	O	T	V	Y	D	B	C	F	C	M	B	R	O	G	Q
I	V	O	J	S	D	W	S	E	V	I	H	Y	A	H	K	H	R	N	S
V	D	I	T	T	Y	A	N	T	T	D	T	M	N	H	C	H	A	S	H
E	W	E	R	H	X	B	D	S	P	S	T	R	E	A	M	H	D	E	F
T	L	R	B	G	E	Z	C	D	U	E	N	A	E	W	J	T	N	H	L
F	H	U	B	O	I	R	F	G	Y	O	A	P	P	G	P	V	E	C	X
A	O	T	F	J	R	N	U	H	S	W	L	N	Q	R	R	J	L	A	M
I	N	C	Y	A	E	A	I	N	E	E	E	D	U	I	I	A	A	O	Y
N	E	I	L	U	N	C	H	A	I	N	S	N	O	T	E	L	C	R	D
T	Y	P	L	L	X	O	B	Y	U	S	R	B	Q	S	S	H	A	E	L
S	L	B	D	V	J	L	F	J	L	I	L	Y	L	A	W	M	P	I	N

ANGRY	DADDY	IMPULSIVE	NEIL	REGRETS
APRIL	DEBORAH	JAR	NOTE	ROACHES
AUGUST	DROWNS	JOHNSON	OPEN	ROSALEEN
BECCA	FAINTS	JUNE	OWENS	SPRINKLER
BEES	FAN	KIDD	PAPER	STEW
BLUE	FONTANEL	LAW	PEACH	STREAM
BOATWRIGHT	FORREST	LILY	PEANUTS	TIBURON
BRACELET	GABRIEL	LOVE	PICTURE	TICA
BUGS	GASTON	MAMA	PIN	TOMATOES
CALENDAR	GRITS	MARY	PINK	VIRGINIA
CHAINS	HENRY	MAY	QUEEN	VOTE
CHARM	HIVES	MISERY	RACE	WAILING
CHICK	HONEY	MOTHER	RAY	ZACH

ANSWER KEY WORD SEARCH: The Secret Life of Bees

B	R	A	C	E	L	E	T	R	C	T	P	K	M	A	Y	G	L	R	
E	G		H		E		E	E	T	H	R	I	I			A	O	A	
E	A		A		N	P	W	L	O	G	I	O	N	D		S	V	Y	Y
S	B	Y	R		A	B	A	K	M	I		C	S	K	D	T	E	R	
I	R	R	M	P	T	E	I	N	A	R	V	T	K	A	W	O	G	N	
M	I	E		F	N	C	L	I	T	W		O	I	E	L	N	E	E	
P	E	S	G	O	O	C	I	R	O	T			T	B	A	E		P	
U	L	I	D	R	F	A	N	P	E	A	Z	S		E	U	B	E	O	
L		M		R	E		G	S	S	O		A		Q	A	R	U	N	
S	M			E	O	T				B	C		C	M			O	G	
I	V	O		S	D	W	S	E	V	I	H		A	H		H	R	N	S
V	D	I	T	T		A	N		T		T	M			C		A	S	
E		E	R	H			D	S	P	S	T	R	E	A	M		D	E	
		R	B	G	E			D	U	E	N	A	E				N	H	
F	H	U		O	I	R		G	Y	O	A	P	P	G			E	C	
A	O	T	F		R	N	U	H	S	W		N		R	R	J	L	A	
I	N	C		A	E	A	I	N	E	E	E		U	I	I	A	A	O	Y
N	E	I	L	U	N	C	H	A	I	N	S	N	O	T	E	L	C	R	
T	Y	P	L			O			U	S	R			S	S		A	E	
S		B			J			J	L	I	L	Y	L	A	W	M	P	I	N

ANGRY	DADDY	IMPULSIVE	NEIL	REGRETS
APRIL	DEBORAH	JAR	NOTE	ROACHES
AUGUST	DROWNS	JOHNSON	OPEN	ROSALEEN
BECCA	FAINTS	JUNE	OWENS	SPRINKLER
BEES	FAN	KIDD	PAPER	STEW
BLUE	FONTANEL	LAW	PEACH	STREAM
BOATWRIGHT	FORREST	LILY	PEANUTS	TIBURON
BRACELET	GABRIEL	LOVE	PICTURE	TICA
BUGS	GASTON	MAMA	PIN	TOMATOES
CALENDAR	GRITS	MARY	PINK	VIRGINIA
CHAINS	HENRY	MAY	QUEEN	VOTE
CHARM	HIVES	MISERY	RACE	WAILING
CHICK	HONEY	MOTHER	RAY	ZACH

MATCHING 1 *The Secret Life of Bees*

____ 1.	LILY	A.	May's song: O! ___
____ 2.	MARY	B.	Lily's mother
____ 3.	ZACH	C.	He wants to marry June.
____ 4.	FORREST	D.	Lily helped her escape.
____ 5.	FONTANEL	E.	Compassionate and sensible bee-keeper
____ 6.	GABRIEL	F.	The black ___ picture led Lily to August.
____ 7.	BECCA	G.	Daughters of ___
____ 8.	MAMA	H.	Lily's mother's maiden name
____ 9.	AUGUST	I.	Lily's father; T. ___
____ 10.	NEIL	J.	Lily says he is one-third friend, one-third brother, one-third bee partner, & one-third boyfriend.
____ 11.	APRIL	K.	Musician who resents Lily
____ 12.	ROSALEEN	L.	She ran away from home.
____ 13.	RAY	M.	She lacks built-in protection around her heart.
____ 14.	DEBORAH	N.	This President signed the Civil Rights Act into law.
____ 15.	VIRGINIA	O.	Home state of Deborah and August
____ 16.	MADONNA	P.	Clayton Forrest's daughter
____ 17.	JOHNSON	Q.	In every picture, he had a big white lily for Mary.
____ 18.	SUSANNA	R.	Boatwrights' grandmother: Big ___
____ 19.	MAY	S.	She committed suicide at age 15.
____ 20.	JUNE	T.	Lily calls T. Ray from his office.

MATCHING 1 ANSWER KEY *The Secret Life of Bees*

L	1. LILY	A.	May's song: O! ___
G	2. MARY	B.	Lily's mother
J	3. ZACH	C.	He wants to marry June.
T	4. FORREST	D.	Lily helped her escape.
H	5. FONTANEL	E.	Compassionate and sensible bee-keeper
Q	6. GABRIEL	F.	The black ___ picture led Lily to August.
P	7. BECCA	G.	Daughters of ___
R	8. MAMA	H.	Lily's mother's maiden name
E	9. AUGUST	I.	Lily's father; T. ___
C	10. NEIL	J.	Lily says he is one-third friend, one-third brother, one-third bee partner, & one-third boyfriend.
S	11. APRIL	K.	Musician who resents Lily
D	12. ROSALEEN	L.	She ran away from home.
I	13. RAY	M.	She lacks built-in protection around her heart.
B	14. DEBORAH	N.	This President signed the Civil Rights Act into law.
O	15. VIRGINIA	O.	Home state of Deborah and August
F	16. MADONNA	P.	Clayton Forrest's daughter
N	17. JOHNSON	Q.	In every picture, he had a big white lily for Mary.
A	18. SUSANNA	R.	Boatwrights' grandmother: Big ___
M	19. MAY	S.	She committed suicide at age 15.
K	20. JUNE	T.	Lily calls T. Ray from his office.

MATCHING 2 *The Secret Life of Bees*

____ 1.	PICTURE	A.	The stone wall is May's ___ wall.
____ 2.	ORCHARD	B.	Lily Melissa Owens, your jar is ___.
____ 3.	BRACELET	C.	Nickname for the Boatwrights: ___ sisters
____ 4.	JOHNSON	D.	May left one for August and June.
____ 5.	PEACH	E.	T. Ray makes Lily kneel on these.
____ 6.	MADONNA	F.	Lily's place of peace and comfort
____ 7.	BUGS	G.	This President signed the Civil Rights Act into law.
____ 8.	CHICK	H.	You ain't touchin' that ___.
____ 9.	CHARM	I.	June and Lily wrestle over it.
____ 10.	GRITS	J.	Our Lady of ___
____ 11.	VOTE	K.	Rosaleen wants to register to do this.
____ 12.	CALENDAR	L.	Deborah was a lunatic when it came to saving these.
____ 13.	NOTE	M.	August covered them with black cloths after May died.
____ 14.	HIVES	N.	August's last name
____ 15.	CHAINS	O.	The black ___ picture led Lily to August.
____ 16.	WAILING	P.	Bee yard etiquette says you should send the bees this.
____ 17.	LOVE	Q.	The most important item in the hat box
____ 18.	BOATWRIGHT	R.	Birthday present Lily wants: charm ___
____ 19.	OPEN	S.	Lily thinks this school will give her a real chance to be beautiful and fashionable.
____ 20.	SPRINKLER	T.	Place where Lily worked: ___ stand

MATCHING 2 ANSWER KEY *The Secret Life of Bees*

Answer	No.	Word	Clue
Q	1.	PICTURE	A. The stone wall is May's ___ wall.
F	2.	ORCHARD	B. Lily Melissa Owens, your jar is ___.
R	3.	BRACELET	C. Nickname for the Boatwrights: ___ sisters
G	4.	JOHNSON	D. May left one for August and June.
T	5.	PEACH	E. T. Ray makes Lily kneel on these.
O	6.	MADONNA	F. Lily's place of peace and comfort
L	7.	BUGS	G. This President signed the Civil Rights Act into law.
H	8.	CHICK	H. You ain't touchin' that ___.
S	9.	CHARM	I. June and Lily wrestle over it.
E	10.	GRITS	J. Our Lady of ___
K	11.	VOTE	K. Rosaleen wants to register to do this.
C	12.	CALENDAR	L. Deborah was a lunatic when it came to saving these.
D	13.	NOTE	M. August covered them with black cloths after May died.
M	14.	HIVES	N. August's last name
J	15.	CHAINS	O. The black ___ picture led Lily to August.
A	16.	WAILING	P. Bee yard etiquette says you should send the bees this.
P	17.	LOVE	Q. The most important item in the hat box
N	18.	BOATWRIGHT	R. Birthday present Lily wants: charm ___
B	19.	OPEN	S. Lily thinks this school will give her a real chance to be beautiful and fashionable.
I	20.	SPRINKLER	T. Place where Lily worked: ___ stand

JUGGLE LETTERS 1 *The Secret Life of Bees*

_______________ = 1. ASLEOREN
Lily helped her escape.

_______________ = 2. DNSOWR
How May dies

_______________ = 3. ANDLCREA
Nickname for the Boatwrights: ___ sisters

_______________ = 4. ALEIBGR
In every picture, he had a big white lily for Mary.

_______________ = 5. TUCIPRE
The most important item in the hat box

_______________ = 6. IEYMRS
Both of us, it seemed, were doomed to ___.

_______________ = 7. RGRTESE
___ don't help anything. You know that.

_______________ = 8. RKLEISPNR
June and Lily wrestle over it.

_______________ = 9. OOTONKBE
Zach's gift to Lily

_______________ = 10. FOLATNNE
Lily's mother's maiden name

_______________ = 11. SAOECHR
May and Deborah lured these out of the house with graham cracker & marshmallow crumbs.

_______________ = 12. RBEAOHD
Lily's mother

_______________ = 13. SJNONHO
This President signed the Civil Rights Act into law.

_______________ = 14. ECBTLREA
Birthday present Lily wants: charm ___

_______________ = 15. ROCRDAH
Lily's place of peace and comfort

_______________ = 16. ONRITBU
Written on back of the black Madonna picture: ___ S.C.

_______________ = 17. HIBRAGTTOW
August's last name

_______________ = 18. WNAIGLI
The stone wall is May's ___ wall.

_______________ = 19. OOAMTETS
June throws these at Neil.

_______________ = 20. MVSILPIUE
Trait common to Lily and Deborah

JUGGLE LETTERS 1 ANSWER KEY *The Secret Life of Bees*

ROSALEEN	= 1.	ASLEOREN Lily helped her escape.
DROWNS	= 2.	DNSOWR How May dies
CALENDAR	= 3.	ANDLCREA Nickname for the Boatwrights: ___ sisters
GABRIEL	= 4.	ALEIBGR In every picture, he had a big white lily for Mary.
PICTURE	= 5.	TUCIPRE The most important item in the hat box
MISERY	= 6.	IEYMRS Both of us, it seemed, were doomed to ___.
REGRETS	= 7.	RGRTESE ___ don't help anything. You know that.
SPRINKLER	= 8.	RKLEISPNR June and Lily wrestle over it.
NOTEBOOK	= 9.	OOTONKBE Zach's gift to Lily
FONTANEL	= 10.	FOLATNNE Lily's mother's maiden name
ROACHES	= 11.	SAOECHR May and Deborah lured these out of the house with graham cracker & marshmallow crumbs.
DEBORAH	= 12.	RBEAOHD Lily's mother
JOHNSON	= 13.	SJNONHO This President signed the Civil Rights Act into law.
BRACELET	= 14.	ECBTLREA Birthday present Lily wants: charm ___
ORCHARD	= 15.	ROCRDAH Lily's place of peace and comfort
TIBURON	= 16.	ONRITBU Written on back of the black Madonna picture: ___ S.C.
BOATWRIGHT	= 17.	HIBRAGTTOW August's last name
WAILING	= 18.	WNAIGLI The stone wall is May's ___ wall.
TOMATOES	= 19.	OOAMTETS June throws these at Neil.
IMPULSIVE	= 20.	MVSILPIUE Trait common to Lily and Deborah

JUGGLE LETTERS 2 *The Secret Life of Bees*

_______________ = 1. SLPMUVIIE
Trait common to Lily and Deborah

_______________ = 2. STMEAR
Place where Lily and Rosaleen reunite

_______________ = 3. TUINBOR
Written on back of the black Madonna picture: ___ S.C.

_______________ = 4. OESNW
Lily's last name

_______________ = 5. GSNOAT
He tells Lily to hush when Rosaleen is struck with the flashlight.

_______________ = 6. CAHEP
Place where Lily worked: ___ stand

_______________ = 7. NMNOADA
The black ___ picture led Lily to August.

_______________ = 8. NIGARIVI
Home state of Deborah and August

_______________ = 9. CKIHC
You ain't touchin' that ___.

_______________ = 10. TIANFS
Lily does this the first time she tries to touch Our Lady's heart.

_______________ = 11. EOTMRH
The Queen bee is this to every bee in the hive.

_______________ = 12. TPNEUSA
August and Lily like this in their Coke.

_______________ = 13. PRCTEIU
The most important item in the hat box

_______________ = 14. DARANELC
Nickname for the Boatwrights: ___ sisters

_______________ = 15. IVESH
August covered them with black cloths after May died.

_______________ = 16. ONRSWD
How May dies

_______________ = 17. FLETNNAO
Lily's mother's maiden name

_______________ = 18. ROAHSEC
May and Deborah lured these out of the house with graham cracker & marshmallow crumbs.

_______________ = 19. ROFTSRE
Lily calls T. Ray from his office.

_______________ = 20. AORLEENS
Lily helped her escape.

JUGGLE LETTERS 2 ANSWER KEY *The Secret Life of Bees*

IMPULSIVE = 1. SLPMUVIIE
Trait common to Lily and Deborah

STREAM = 2. STMEAR
Place where Lily and Rosaleen reunite

TIBURON = 3. TUINBOR
Written on back of the black Madonna picture: ___ S.C.

OWENS = 4. OESNW
Lily's last name

GASTON = 5. GSNOAT
He tells Lily to hush when Rosaleen is struck with the flashlight.

PEACH = 6. CAHEP
Place where Lily worked: ___ stand

MADONNA = 7. NMNOADA
The black ___ picture led Lily to August.

VIRGINIA = 8. NIGARIVI
Home state of Deborah and August

CHICK = 9. CKIHC
You ain't touchin' that ___.

FAINTS = 10. TIANFS
Lily does this the first time she tries to touch Our Lady's heart.

MOTHER = 11. EOTMRH
The Queen bee is this to every bee in the hive.

PEANUTS = 12. TPNEUSA
August and Lily like this in their Coke.

PICTURE = 13. PRCTEIU
The most important item in the hat box

CALENDAR = 14. DARANELC
Nickname for the Boatwrights: ___ sisters

HIVES = 15. IVESH
August covered them with black cloths after May died.

DROWNS = 16. ONRSWD
How May dies

FONTANEL = 17. FLETNNAO
Lily's mother's maiden name

ROACHES = 18. ROAHSEC
May and Deborah lured these out of the house with graham cracker & marshmallow crumbs.

FORREST = 19. ROFTSRE
Lily calls T. Ray from his office.

ROSALEEN = 20. AORLEENS
Lily helped her escape.

VOCABULARY RESOURCE MATERIALS

The Secret Life of Bees Vocabulary

No.	Word	Clue/Definition
1.	ACCORDED	Given to
2.	AGITATES	Stirs up
3.	AMNESIAC	Someone who cannot remember
4.	APTITUDE	Natural talent or ability
5.	ARRAY	Large number or variety
6.	ASCRIBED	Attributed to a particular cause, source, or origin
7.	BILLOWS	Rolling clusters of something such as smoke
8.	BLASPHEME	Speak of something sacred in an irreverent manner
9.	BORDELLO	House of prostitution
10.	BRAZEN	Bold
11.	CAPABLE	Able; competent
12.	CAROUSING	Drunken merrymaking
13.	CICADAS	Large, winged insect; males make a high-pitched, droning noise.
14.	CLOISTER	Place of religious seclusion and meditation
15.	COAX	Gently persuade
16.	CONCOCT	Invent; make up
17.	CONJURE	Create from nothing, as if by magic
18.	CONSOLATION	Comfort; cheer in a time of grief, defeat, or trouble
19.	CONTEMPTIBLE	Undeserving of respect
20.	CREVICE	Narrow crack
21.	DESPICABLE	Horrible; deserving only contempt
22.	DRONES	Male bees that mate with the queen
23.	ECLECTIC	Made up of elements from several unlike sources
24.	ELIMINATED	Got rid of
25.	ELUSIVE	Difficult to find, catch, or understand
26.	EXCRUCIATING	Extremely painful
27.	EXCURSION	Short trip
28.	EXORCISM	Process of releasing evil spirits from a place or person
29.	FLOUNCED	Moved with exaggerated motions expressive of displeasure or impatience
30.	FORAGING	Searching for food
31.	FORFEITED	Gave up something willingly
32.	GEYSER	Spring that regularly, forcefully ejects a stream of hot water or steam up into the air
33.	GOUGED	Cut or scooped holes in something
34.	HIGHBROW	Cultural and intellectual
35.	HILARITY	Extreme funniness
36.	IMMUNITY	Exemption or protection from danger
37.	INDIGNATION	Anger due to injustice or unreasonable action
38.	INDUCTION	Process of introducing someone to a group

No.	Word	Clue/Definition
39.	INDUSTRIOUS	Hard-working
40.	INFERNO	Place of a fiercely burning fire
41.	INGENIOUS	Clever and original
42.	INNATE	Possessed at birth; inborn
43.	KEEL	Collapse or fall
44.	LAMENT	Expression of grief
45.	LOAFING	Spending time in a lazy way
46.	LOPING	Characterized by long, easy strides
47.	LURING	Offering something tempting in order to persuade
48.	MEANDER	Moved casually and leisurely, with no direct route
49.	MELANCHOLY	With a gentle sadness
50.	MINISCULE	Tiny
51.	MUDDLED	Confused
52.	MULL	Consider; think deeply about
53.	NEUROTIC	Overanxious or oversensitive about trivial occurrences
54.	NUMB	Without feeling
55.	OBLIVIOUS	Completely unaware
56.	ORNERINESS	Stubborn and irritable attitude
57.	PATENTED	Registered as one's own unique idea, process, or product
58.	PERPETUALLY	Continually; always; without end
59.	PIOUS	Deeply religious
60.	PRESUMPTUOUS	Excessively forward or confident
61.	PULSATING	Expanding and contracting in a certain pattern
62.	RECEDE	Lessen or become distant
63.	REMNANTS	Small leftover amounts
64.	REVELATON	Newly-discovered information, especially surprising information
65.	RILED	Provoked to anger
66.	RIOTOUS	Loud, unrestrained behavior
67.	SALVATION	Preservation or deliverance from evil or difficulty
68.	SASHAYING	Walking with a sway of the hips that intends to attract attention
69.	SERENADE	Sing or perform a moving musical piece for a specific person
70.	SHACKLED	Chained
71.	SHIFTLESS	Lazy
72.	SKITTISH	Easily frightened
73.	SNAGGED	Caught by a sharp point
74.	SNUFF	Tobacco in the form of powder, taken by sniffing it
75.	SPECTACLE	Something to be witnessed because of its impressive nature
76.	SPEWING	Forcing out in a stream
77.	UNPERTURBED	Not disturbed; not bothered; unruffled
78.	VIGIL	An all-night event spent watching, praying, or guarding

No.	Word	Clue/Definition
79.	VIGILANTE	Those who punish lawbreakers themselves instead of relying upon official legal authority
80.	WAFTED	Moved or floated gently through the air
81.	YOKE	Device encircling the necks of a pair of oxen, mules, or other draft animals walking in a team; a restrictive or repressive force

VOCABULARY CROSSWORD - The Secret Life of Bees

Across
2. Clever or original
3. Tobacco in the form of powder, taken by sniffing it
5. Someone who cannot remember
8. Expression of grief
10. Large number or variety
12. House of prostitution
15. Device encircling the necks of a pair of draft animals; a restrictive or repressive force
16. Collapse or fall
18. Moved or floated gently through the air
19. Provoked to anger
20. Without feeling
21. Overanxious or oversensitive about trivial occurrences

Down
1. Consider; think deeply about
2. Possessed at birth; inborn
3. Forcing out in a stream
4. Gave up something willingly
5. Attributed to a particular cause or source
6. Caught by a sharp point
7. Gently persuade
9. Given to
11. Cut or scooped holes in something
13. Loud, unrestrained behavior
14. Spending time in a lazy way
17. An all-night event spent watching, praying, or guarding

ANSWER KEY VOCABULARY CROSSWORD - The Secret Life of Bees

									1 M							
		2 I	N	G	E	N	I	O	U	S		3 S	N	U	F	4 F
		N							L			P				O
5 A	M	N	E	6 S	I	A	7 C		8 L	9 A	M	E	N	T		R
S		A		N			O			C		W				F
C		T		10 A	R	R	A	Y		C		I				E
R		E		G			X			O		N				I
I				G						R		G		11 G		T
12 B	O	13 R	D	E	L	14 L	O			D			15 Y	O	K	E
E		I		D		O		16 K	E	E	L			U		D
D		O				A				D		17 V		G		
		T		18 W	A	F	T	E	D		19 R	I	L	E	D	
		O				I						G		D		
	20 N	U	M	B		21 N	E	U	R	O	T	I	C			
		S				G						L				

Across
2. Clever or original
3. Tobacco in the form of powder, taken by sniffing it
5. Someone who cannot remember
8. Expression of grief
10. Large number or variety
12. House of prostitution
15. Device encircling the necks of a pair of draft animals; a restrictive or repressive force
16. Collapse or fall
18. Moved or floated gently through the air
19. Provoked to anger
20. Without feeling
21. Overanxious or oversensitive about trivial occurrences

Down
1. Consider; think deeply about
2. Possessed at birth; inborn
3. Forcing out in a stream
4. Gave up something willingly
5. Attributed to a particular cause or source
6. Caught by a sharp point
7. Gently persuade
9. Given to
11. Cut or scooped holes in something
13. Loud, unrestrained behavior
14. Spending time in a lazy way
17. An all-night event spent watching, praying, or guarding

VOCABULARY WORD SEARCH - The Secret Life of Bees

E	X	C	R	U	C	I	A	T	I	N	G	R	I	O	T	O	U	S	N
G	N	Z	E	Z	C	I	N	G	E	N	I	O	U	S	N	F	G	T	K
V	K	M	D	J	O	F	P	S	S	E	N	I	R	E	N	R	O	N	Z
F	Q	U	N	S	N	A	G	G	E	D	N	A	Z	T	N	B	C	A	X
O	H	D	A	J	S	G	J	J	Y	E	E	A	T	N	D	I	C	N	T
Y	B	D	E	P	O	T	P	Q	U	D	R	W	Z	E	C	L	F	M	J
J	S	L	M	F	L	S	Q	R	V	B	U	C	V	M	I	L	L	E	H
C	L	E	I	B	A	G	O	F	P	N	J	Q	D	A	C	O	O	R	V
F	F	D	Z	V	T	T	Y	C	W	I	N	R	M	L	A	W	U	G	P
K	E	D	U	T	I	T	P	A	C	C	O	R	D	E	D	S	N	N	Q
E	E	G	Z	C	O	O	F	Q	M	N	C	U	C	M	A	I	C	U	B
M	C	E	E	S	N	T	U	S	E	N	H	R	S	D	S	D	E	M	M
M	U	L	L	Y	E	P	H	S	N	I	E	D	E	U	N	E	D	B	X
R	V	O	E	D	S	R	M	I	L	U	E	S	O	V	V	W	O	A	X
E	I	A	G	C	Z	E	E	A	G	B	F	R	I	I	I	N	O	G	P
C	G	F	O	A	T	M	R	N	I	H	A	F	S	A	R	C	N	R	G
E	I	I	U	K	R	I	I	R	A	C	B	U	D	E	C	I	E	I	W
D	L	N	G	P	T	R	C	J	B	D	L	R	F	S	P	W	K	L	T
E	S	G	E	Y	U	S	A	F	M	E	E	N	O	O	J	X	O	E	G
M	V	V	D	L	A	V	Q	Y	C	F	I	D	L	W	N	G	Y	D	J

ACCORDED	CREVICE	INNATE	ORNERINESS
AMNESIAC	DRONES	KEEL	PIOUS
APTITUDE	ECLECTIC	LAMENT	RECEDE
ARRAY	ELUSIVE	LOAFING	REMNANTS
ASCRIBED	EXCRUCIATING	LOPING	RILED
BILLOWS	FLOUNCED	LURING	RIOTOUS
BRAZEN	GEYSER	MEANDER	SERENADE
CAROUSING	GOUGED	MUDDLED	SNAGGED
CICADAS	HIGHBROW	MULL	SNUFF
COAX	HILARITY	NEUROTIC	VIGIL
CONJURE	INFERNO	NUMB	WAFTED
CONSOLATION	INGENIOUS	OBLIVIOUS	YOKE

ANSWER KEY VOCABULARY WORD SEARCH - The Secret Life of Bees

E	X	C	R	U	C	I	A	T	I	N	G	R	I	O	T	O	U	S	
			E		C	I	N	G	E	N	I	O	U	S	N			T	
		M	D		O			S	S	E	N	I	R	E	N	R	O	N	
		U	N	S	N	A	G	G	E	D	N	A	Z	T		B		A	
O		D	A		S					E	E	A	T	N		I		N	
	B	D	E		O				U		R			E	C	L	F	M	
		L	M		L			R		B	U			M	I	L	L	E	
		E	I		A		O		P		J		D	A	C	O	O	R	
		D		V	T	T			W	I	N	R		L	A	W	U	G	
K	E	D	U	T	I	T	P	A	C	C	O	R	D	E	D	S	N	N	
E	E	G		C	O	O	F		M	N	C	U			A	I	C	U	
	C	E	E	S	N	T	U	S	E	N	H	R	S		S		E	M	
M	U	L	L	Y	E		H	S	N	I	E	D	E	U		E	D	B	X
R	V	O	E	D	S	R		I	L	U	E	S	O	V	V		O	A	
E	I	A	G	C		E	E	A	G	B	F	R	I	I	I	N	O	G	
C	G	F	O	A	T		R	N	I	H	A	F	S	A	R	C	N	R	
E	I	I	U		R	I	I	R	A	C	B	U		E	C	I	E	I	
D	L	N	G		T	R	C			D	L	R	F		P		K	L	
E		G	E	Y	U	S	A			E	E	N	O	O			O	E	
			D	L	A			Y			I		L	W			Y	D	

ACCORDED
AMNESIAC
APTITUDE
ARRAY
ASCRIBED
BILLOWS
BRAZEN
CAROUSING
CICADAS
COAX
CONJURE
CONSOLATION

CREVICE
DRONES
ECLECTIC
ELUSIVE
EXCRUCIATING
FLOUNCED
GEYSER
GOUGED
HIGHBROW
HILARITY
INFERNO
INGENIOUS

INNATE
KEEL
LAMENT
LOAFING
LOPING
LURING
MEANDER
MUDDLED
MULL
NEUROTIC
NUMB
OBLIVIOUS

ORNERINESS
PIOUS
RECEDE
REMNANTS
RILED
RIOTOUS
SERENADE
SNAGGED
SNUFF
VIGIL
WAFTED
YOKE

VOCABULARY MATCHING 1 *The Secret Life of Bees*

____ 1.	ACCORDED	A.	Those who punish lawbreakers themselves instead of relying upon official legal authority
____ 2.	HIGHBROW	B.	Given to
____ 3.	INDUCTION	C.	With a gentle sadness
____ 4.	INFERNO	D.	Able; competent
____ 5.	LOPING	E.	Invent; make up
____ 6.	MELANCHOLY	F.	Characterized by long, easy strides
____ 7.	MINISCULE	G.	Gave up something willingly
____ 8.	PRESUMPTUOUS	H.	Expanding and contracting in a certain pattern
____ 9.	PULSATING	I.	Speak of something sacred in an irreverent manner
____ 10.	FORFEITED	J.	Male bees that mate with the queen
____ 11.	EXCRUCIATING	K.	Cultural and intellectual
____ 12.	AMNESIAC	L.	Place of a fiercely burning fire
____ 13.	ASCRIBED	M.	Extremely painful
____ 14.	BLASPHEME	N.	Undeserving of respect
____ 15.	CAPABLE	O.	Someone who cannot remember
____ 16.	CICADAS	P.	Tiny
____ 17.	CONCOCT	Q.	Process of introducing someone to a group
____ 18.	CONTEMPTIBLE	R.	Attributed to a particular cause, source, or origin
____ 19.	DRONES	S.	Excessively forward or confident
____ 20.	VIGILANTE	T.	Large, winged insect; males make a high-pitched, droning noise.

VOCABULARY MATCHING 1 ANSWER KEY *The Secret Life of Bees*

B	1.	ACCORDED	A.	Those who punish lawbreakers themselves instead of relying upon official legal authority
K	2.	HIGHBROW	B.	Given to
Q	3.	INDUCTION	C.	With a gentle sadness
L	4.	INFERNO	D.	Able; competent
F	5.	LOPING	E.	Invent; make up
C	6.	MELANCHOLY	F.	Characterized by long, easy strides
P	7.	MINISCULE	G.	Gave up something willingly
S	8.	PRESUMPTUOUS	H.	Expanding and contracting in a certain pattern
H	9.	PULSATING	I.	Speak of something sacred in an irreverent manner
G	10.	FORFEITED	J.	Male bees that mate with the queen
M	11.	EXCRUCIATING	K.	Cultural and intellectual
O	12.	AMNESIAC	L.	Place of a fiercely burning fire
R	13.	ASCRIBED	M.	Extremely painful
I	14.	BLASPHEME	N.	Undeserving of respect
D	15.	CAPABLE	O.	Someone who cannot remember
T	16.	CICADAS	P.	Tiny
E	17.	CONCOCT	Q.	Process of introducing someone to a group
N	18.	CONTEMPTIBLE	R.	Attributed to a particular cause, source, or origin
J	19.	DRONES	S.	Excessively forward or confident
A	20.	VIGILANTE	T.	Large, winged insect; males make a high-pitched, droning noise.

VOCABULARY MATCHING 2 *The Secret Life of Bees*

____	1.	CONJURE	A.	Stubborn and irritable attitude
____	2.	PERPETUALLY	B.	Expanding and contracting in a certain pattern
____	3.	PULSATING	C.	Registered as one's own unique idea, process, or product
____	4.	REMNANTS	D.	Device encircling the necks of a pair of oxen, mules, or other draft animals walking in a team; a restrictive or repressive force
____	5.	RIOTOUS	E.	Expression of grief
____	6.	SALVATION	F.	Caught by a sharp point
____	7.	SERENADE	G.	Small leftover amounts
____	8.	SNAGGED	H.	Male bees that mate with the queen
____	9.	UNPERTURBED	I.	Without feeling
____	10.	PATENTED	J.	Extreme funniness
____	11.	ORNERINESS	K.	Spring that regularly, forcefully ejects a stream of hot water or steam up into the air
____	12.	DRONES	L.	Loud, unrestrained behavior
____	13.	GEYSER	M.	Confused
____	14.	HILARITY	N.	Process of introducing someone to a group
____	15.	INDIGNATION	O.	Create from nothing, as if by magic
____	16.	INDUCTION	P.	Continually; always; without end
____	17.	LAMENT	Q.	Sing or perform a moving musical piece for a specific person
____	18.	MUDDLED	R.	Not disturbed; not bothered; unruffled
____	19.	NUMB	S.	Anger due to injustice or unreasonable action
____	20.	YOKE	T.	Preservation or deliverance from evil or difficulty

VOCABULARY MATCHING 2 ANSWER KEY *The Secret Life of Bees*

Answer	Word	Definition
O	1. CONJURE	A. Stubborn and irritable attitude
P	2. PERPETUALLY	B. Expanding and contracting in a certain pattern
B	3. PULSATING	C. Registered as one's own unique idea, process, or product
G	4. REMNANTS	D. Device encircling the necks of a pair of oxen, mules, or other draft animals walking in a team; a restrictive or repressive force
L	5. RIOTOUS	E. Expression of grief
T	6. SALVATION	F. Caught by a sharp point
Q	7. SERENADE	G. Small leftover amounts
F	8. SNAGGED	H. Male bees that mate with the queen
R	9. UNPERTURBED	I. Without feeling
C	10. PATENTED	J. Extreme funniness
A	11. ORNERINESS	K. Spring that regularly, forcefully ejects a stream of hot water or steam up into the air
H	12. DRONES	L. Loud, unrestrained behavior
K	13. GEYSER	M. Confused
J	14. HILARITY	N. Process of introducing someone to a group
S	15. INDIGNATION	O. Create from nothing, as if by magic
N	16. INDUCTION	P. Continually; always; without end
E	17. LAMENT	Q. Sing or perform a moving musical piece for a specific person
M	18. MUDDLED	R. Not disturbed; not bothered; unruffled
I	19. NUMB	S. Anger due to injustice or unreasonable action
D	20. YOKE	T. Preservation or deliverance from evil or difficulty

VOCABULARY JUGGLE LETTERS 1 *The Secret Life of Bees*

_______________ = 1. AWETDF
Moved or floated gently through the air

_______________ = 2. NIITDOGANNI
Anger due to injustice or unreasonable action

_______________ = 3. CMIESRXO
Process of releasing evil spirits from a place or person

_______________ = 4. IDAILMETEN
Got rid of

_______________ = 5. CTLICCEE
Made up of elements from several unlike sources

_______________ = 6. SBCIPELDAE
Horrible; deserving only contempt

_______________ = 7. ISOUAGRNC
Drunken merrymaking

_______________ = 8. BLPEESMHA
Speak of something sacred in an irreverent manner

_______________ = 9. TTAUPEDI
Natural talent or ability

_______________ = 10. ANETIN
Possessed at birth; inborn

_______________ = 11. EAMDNER
Moved casually and leisurely, with no direct route

_______________ = 12. EDURPBTUERN
Not disturbed; not bothered; unruffled

_______________ = 13. EPCLEACST
Something to be witnessed because of its impressive nature

_______________ = 14. KLEADHCS
Chained

_______________ = 15. ROUOSIT
Loud, unrestrained behavior

_______________ = 16. TRNLEVEOA
Newly-discovered information, especially surprising information

_______________ = 17. MRPUUPUSSTOE
Excessively forward or confident

_______________ = 18. CEUOITNR
Overanxious or oversensitive about trivial occurrences

_______________ = 19. DLMEDDU
Confused

_______________ = 20. TESTAGIA
Stirs up

VOCABULARY JUGGLE LETTERS 1 ANSWER KEY *The Secret Life of Bees*

WAFTED	= 1.	AWETDF Moved or floated gently through the air
INDIGNATION	= 2.	NIITDOGANNI Anger due to injustice or unreasonable action
EXORCISM	= 3.	CMIESRXO Process of releasing evil spirits from a place or person
ELIMINATED	= 4.	IDAILMETEN Got rid of
ECLECTIC	= 5.	CTLICCEE Made up of elements from several unlike sources
DESPICABLE	= 6.	SBCIPELDAE Horrible; deserving only contempt
CAROUSING	= 7.	ISOUAGRNC Drunken merrymaking
BLASPHEME	= 8.	BLPEESMHA Speak of something sacred in an irreverent manner
APTITUDE	= 9.	TTAUPEDI Natural talent or ability
INNATE	= 10.	ANETIN Possessed at birth; inborn
MEANDER	= 11.	EAMDNER Moved casually and leisurely, with no direct route
UNPERTURBED	= 12.	EDURPBTUERN Not disturbed; not bothered; unruffled
SPECTACLE	= 13.	EPCLEACST Something to be witnessed because of its impressive nature
SHACKLED	= 14.	KLEADHCS Chained
RIOTOUS	= 15.	ROUOSIT Loud, unrestrained behavior
REVELATON	= 16.	TRNLEVEOA Newly-discovered information, especially surprising information
PRESUMPTUOUS	= 17.	MRPUUPUSSTOE Excessively forward or confident
NEUROTIC	= 18.	CEUOITNR Overanxious or oversensitive about trivial occurrences
MUDDLED	= 19.	DLMEDDU Confused
AGITATES	= 20.	TESTAGIA Stirs up

VOCABULARY JUGGLE LETTERS 2 *The Secret Life of Bees*

________________ = 1. IMCNEAAS
Someone who cannot remember

________________ = 2. ATEMNL
Expression of grief

________________ = 3. DMERANE
Moved casually and leisurely, with no direct route

________________ = 4. BUISVILOO
Completely unaware

________________ = 5. TUNPSIGLA
Expanding and contracting in a certain pattern

________________ = 6. DRECEE
Lessen or become distant

________________ = 7. SSNHIGAAY
Walking with a sway of the hips that intends to attract attention

________________ = 8. SIISTHTK
Easily frightened

________________ = 9. IWSEGNP
Forcing out in a stream

________________ = 10. REOINNF
Place of a fiercely burning fire

________________ = 11. OEDGUG
Cut or scooped holes in something

________________ = 12. ECRADBSI
Attributed to a particular cause, source, or origin

________________ = 13. ACSDIAC
Large, winged insect; males make a high-pitched, droning noise

________________ = 14. XCAO
Gently persuade

________________ = 15. TSINOOCONLA
Comfort; cheer in a time of grief, defeat, or trouble

________________ = 16. CELTCCEI
Made up of elements from several unlike sources

________________ = 17. DLEETNIIAM
Got rid of

________________ = 18. ISRONXEUC
Short trip

________________ = 19. GGRFONIA
Searching for food

________________ = 20. VIGIL
An all-night event spent watching, praying, or guarding

VOCABULARY JUGGLE LETTERS 2 ANSWER KEY *The Secret Life of Bees*

AMNESIAC	= 1.	IMCNEAAS Someone who cannot remember
LAMENT	= 2.	ATEMNL Expression of grief
MEANDER	= 3.	DMERANE Moved casually and leisurely, with no direct route
OBLIVIOUS	= 4.	BUISVILOO Completely unaware
PULSATING	= 5.	TUNPSIGLA Expanding and contracting in a certain pattern
RECEDE	= 6.	DRECEE Lessen or become distant
SASHAYING	= 7.	SSNHIGAAY Walking with a sway of the hips that intends to attract attention
SKITTISH	= 8.	SIISTHTK Easily frightened
SPEWING	= 9.	IWSEGNP Forcing out in a stream
INFERNO	= 10.	REOINNF Place of a fiercely burning fire
GOUGED	= 11.	OEDGUG Cut or scooped holes in something
ASCRIBED	= 12.	ECRADBSI Attributed to a particular cause, source, or origin
CICADAS	= 13.	ACSDIAC Large, winged insect; males make a high-pitched, droning noise
COAX	= 14.	XCAO Gently persuade
CONSOLATION	= 15.	TSINOOCONLA Comfort; cheer in a time of grief, defeat, or trouble
ECLECTIC	= 16.	CELTCCEI Made up of elements from several unlike sources
ELIMINATED	= 17.	DLEETNIIAM Got rid of
EXCURSION	= 18.	ISRONXEUC Short trip
FORAGING	= 19.	GGRFONIA Searching for food
VIGIL	= 20.	VIGIL An all-night event spent watching, praying, or guarding

www.ingramcontent.com/pod-product-compliance
Lightning Source LLC
Chambersburg PA
CBHW082101090726
47910CB00008B/2549
* 9 7 8 1 6 0 2 4 9 0 6 0 4 *